THE SALES TACTICIAN

Spycraft Techniques For Revenue Success

By Mort Greenberg

To every business person that wants to look deeper and continue the search for improving business outcomes, every day of every year, ***this book is dedicated to each of you!***

Copyright © 2025 by Mort Greenberg

Design and Illustrations: Heri Susanto

First Paperback edition March 2025

Print Paperback ISBN: 978-1-961059-13-9
Kindle KPF ISBN: 978-1-961059-14-6
Ingram EPUB ISBN: 978-1-961059-15-3

Published by digitalCORE
www.dgtlcore.com

digitalCORE

Other Books by Mort Greenberg

REVENUE VS. SALES SERIES

- **The Singular Focus**
  100+ Tips to Maximize Your Revenue

- **Revenue Boost**
  The Ultimate Sales Plan in Five Steps

- **Straight Up Selling**
  Your Toolbox for Sales Excellence

THE FOCUSED SELLER SERIES

- **Maximizing Human Performance in Sales**
  Unlocking Your Best Results By Thinking Like A
  Business Owner

- **The Sales Tactician**
  Spycraft Techniques for Revenue Success

- **Elevate**
  Mastering the Art of Sales Leadership

- **Beyond The Acquisition**
  Thriving With Private Equity Ownership

CHILDREN'S BOOK SERIES

The Fearless Girl and The Little Guy with Greatness

- **Book 1** - Live Life Motivated
- **Book 2** - Young Leaders Guide
- **Book 3** - Asking Awesome Questions
- **Book 4** - Think to Win
- **Book 5** - Smart Money Moves
- **Book 6** - Wellness Warriors
- **Book 7** - Travel Like a Pro
- **Book 8** - Outdoor Skills

INTRODUCTION

Welcome to *"The Sales Tactician: Spycraft Techniques for Revenue Success,"* the second installment in "The Focused Seller" series. This book gets into the art and science of applying espionage techniques to enhance your sales strategies. Here, you'll discover how to harness the power of precision, strategy, and psychological insight—skills honed in the world of intelligence—to elevate your sales performance.

In the first book of the series, *"Maximizing Human Performance In Sales: Unlocking Your Best Results By Thinking Like A Business Owner,"* we established the groundwork by adopting a business owner's mindset, focusing on fundamental principles of self-motivation, productivity, and strategic thinking. "The Sales Tactician" builds on these principles by introducing you to the world of spycraft, where every interaction is an opportunity to gather critical data, build trust, and influence outcomes in your favor.

As you enhance your tactical skills with this book, the pathway is set for the next stages in *"The Focused Seller"* series. Following the spycraft and strategic interaction mastery, you will progress to *"Elevate: Mastering the Art of Sales Leadership,"* where the focus shifts to leading and inspiring sales teams, and finally to *"Beyond The Acquisition: Thriving with Private Equity Ownership,"* which prepares you for navigating complex business transitions and maximizing growth under private equity.

Each book in the series is interconnected, offering a step-by-step guide to mastering every aspect of the sales process, from individual performance to leadership and strategic business management. *"The Sales Tactician"* is designed not only to refine your skills but also to act as a bridge between personal sales effectiveness and the broader challenges of sales leadership and organizational success.

Embark on this journey with *"The Sales Tactician"* and prepare to transform your sales approach with the calculated precision of a spy. Unlock the secrets to deeper client relationships, more effective negotiations, and ultimately, unparalleled sales success.

Sales professionals, like clandestine operatives, operate in high-pressure environments where outcomes hinge on their ability to think strategically and act decisively. Both must connect with others, navigate complex dynamics, and adapt to changing circumstances—all while staying focused on their mission. This is the essence of The Sales Tactician: Spycraft Techniques For Revenue Success.

This book bridges the gap between these two worlds, offering a fresh perspective on sales success by drawing on the principles and practices of spies. It's not about spy gadgets or covert missions—it's about understanding human behavior, using observation to uncover hidden insights, and leveraging that knowledge to build trust and guide decisions. The strategies outlined here aren't just theoretical; they're practical, actionable tools designed to help you thrive in the business world.

Whether you're decoding a prospect's body language, reframing objections, or crafting a strategic pitch, the skills you'll learn in this book will elevate your ability to influence and connect. You'll approach each sales interaction with the mindset of an operative—prepared, adaptable, and always one step ahead.

Your mission is clear. Now it's time to execute.

Author's Note

When I began my journey in sales, I quickly realized that success wasn't just about hitting numbers—it was about understanding people, building trust, and navigating challenges with precision and resilience.

Over the years, I've seen the parallels between the discipline of elite intelligence operatives and the skillset required for exceptional sales performance. Both professions demand preparation, adaptability, and the ability to connect with people on a deep level.

The idea for The Sales Tactician: Spycraft Techniques For Revenue Success came from eight plus years working for a publisher in the military, defense and national security space with all types of people in the Department of Defense, Pentagon, Capitol Hill and other government agencies.

What stood out time after time were conversations about methods used by intelligence officers — how operatives gather data, decode behavior, and influence decisions in high-stakes situations. I saw an opportunity to adapt those techniques for the sales world, creating a framework that empowers sales professionals to think like tacticians and act like leaders.

This book is the culmination of years of learning, observing, and applying strategies that work—not just in closing deals, but in building lasting relationships, overcoming setbacks, and leading with integrity. It's a guide for anyone who wants to elevate their sales game, sharpen their mindset, and embrace the role of trusted advisor.

To the readers of this book: whether you're new to sales or a seasoned professional, I hope you find these principles as transformative as I have. The insights shared here are not just about selling—they're about growing as a person, a professional, and a leader.

Sales is an art and a science, but above all, it's a craft. With practice, dedication, and the right tools, you can master it. This book is my contribution to your journey—a roadmap for thinking strategically, acting decisively, and achieving greatness.

Thank you for trusting me to guide you through this process. Your mission is now in your hands. Execute it boldly, and success will follow.

Sincerely,
Mort Greenberg

```
  N W              1 O S   W L 0 T
  P U              0 P 1   U Q 1 1
  S V            1 1 L 0 S V 0 J
  L N            1 1 Q L 1 N G I
  W O            I 1 J W 0 O H U
  U P N          O T I U T P 0 V
  V L P N        P Y O V Y L 1 N
  N Q S P        1 U P N L Q   O
  O P L S        T O L O 1 1   P
  P L W L            P   0     L
  L   U W      P A 1         L   1   Q
  Q   V U      S S 0   1     1     O
  T   N V    L L D 1 0       1     T
  1 T O N    M W K 1 H R K P U     Y W
  0 1 P O    1 U
  H O I
```

Table of Contents

UNDERSTANDING HUMAN BEHAVIOR

Sales is as much about understanding people as it is about presenting a product or service. The first five chapters of this book lay the foundation for becoming a master of human connection, drawing on techniques inspired by operatives who excel at building trust, decoding behavior, and influencing decisions. These chapters introduce the psychological tools and strategies you need to engage clients deeply, uncover their true needs, and foster meaningful relationships.

CHAPTER 1

The Spy Who Sold Me

> *Success in sales begins with observation, persuasion, and trust—the same tools that operatives use to win hearts and minds.*

The world of sales and the world of espionage may seem worlds apart, but when you peel back the layers, the similarities are striking. At their core, both professions rely on observation, persuasion, and trust-building to achieve their objectives. Intelligence officers don't just gather intelligence; they forge connections, identify vulnerabilities, and strategically act to influence outcomes. Similarly, great salespeople don't merely push products—they understand their clients deeply, build trust, and guide decisions in a way that feels natural and mutually beneficial.

This chapter explores these parallels and introduces the foundational skills that will be your compass as you navigate the intersection of spycraft and sales.

Observation:
The Art of Seeing
What Others Miss

Intelligence officers are masters of observation. They notice details others overlook, from a subtle change in tone to a barely perceptible hesitation. This acute awareness helps them understand their targets' motivations, fears, and needs.

In sales, the same principle applies. Imagine you're in a meeting with a potential client. Their words may tell one story, but their body language or the way they react to certain topics might tell another.

Did they hesitate when discussing their budget? Did their tone brighten when you mentioned a competitor's feature? These cues are breadcrumbs, leading you to uncover what truly matters to them.

Example:

A SaaS salesperson noticed a prospect repeatedly mentioning concerns about downtime during a product demo. While they didn't outright say reliability was their top priority, the salesperson picked up on this underlying fear through their tone and repeated questions. By focusing the rest of the pitch on the platform's uptime guarantees and reliability case studies, they secured the deal.

Persuasion:

The Subtle Science

of Influence

Intelligence officers don't strong-arm their targets into cooperation—they persuade them. Through careful elicitation techniques, operatives frame their suggestions in ways that align with their target's self-interest.

In sales, persuasion isn't about manipulation; it's about alignment. It's about understanding your client's goals and showing how your solution helps them achieve those goals. Framing matters—highlighting benefits that resonate emotionally can turn a lukewarm prospect into an enthusiastic buyer.

Example:

A luxury real estate agent used persuasion to sell a high-end property. Instead of merely listing features like "a spacious living room," they reframed it: "This space is perfect for hosting your annual holiday party, where your family and friends can gather comfortably." By painting a picture of the client's desired lifestyle, they made the sale personal and emotionally compelling.

Trust-Building:

The Foundation of Success

For Intelligence officers, trust is non-negotiable. Without it, assets won't share critical intelligence, and missions fail. Building trust takes time, authenticity, and a consistent track record of reliability.

In sales, trust operates similarly. Clients must feel that you understand their needs, have their best interests at heart, and will deliver on your promises. Trust is built through listening, empathy, and follow-through.

Example:

A B2B account manager regularly checked in with a client after closing a deal—not to upsell, but to ensure everything was working smoothly. Over time, this genuine care led the client to renew their contract and recommend the account manager to others in their industry.

Bringing it

All Together

The interplay of observation, persuasion, and trust-building creates a sales strategy that feels more like a conversation than a pitch. A salesperson armed with these skills isn't just a seller—they're a tactician, guiding prospects to their desired outcome while aligning it with the sales goal.

Workshop

Activities

To turn theory into practice, here are some interactive activities:

Activity 1: Observation Practice

1. Pair up with a partner. One person describes a product or service they use frequently (real or fictional).

2. The listener observes not just what is said but how it is said. Pay attention to tone, body language, and word choice.

3. Afterward, the observer shares their impressions about what the speaker seemed to value most. Compare notes to see how accurate the observations were.

Activity 2: Reframing Exercise

1. Take a feature of a product or service you're selling. Write it down in a straightforward, factual way.

    Example: *"This car has a large trunk."*

2. Now reframe it to align with a potential customer's needs.

    Example: *"This car's spacious trunk means you'll have no problem packing everything for your next family road trip."*

3. Share your reframing with a group or partner to refine your messaging.

Activity 3: Trust-Building Scenarios

1. Break into small groups and discuss the following scenario:

    "A client expresses hesitation about working with your company because of a prior bad experience with another vendor in your industry. How do you rebuild their trust?"

2. Each group presents their approach, and the facilitator provides feedback on how to integrate trust-building techniques effectively.

By the end of this chapter and its workshop, you'll begin to see sales through the lens of a tactician— someone who observes carefully, persuades strategically, and builds trust consistently. These skills form the foundation for everything that follows in this guide.

Conclusion

Sales and espionage share a powerful common thread: the ability to observe, influence, and build trust with precision and purpose. Just as intelligence officers rely on their understanding of human nature to achieve their missions, sales professionals can use similar skills to connect with prospects and guide them toward mutually beneficial decisions. As you move forward, keep in mind that successful selling is not about manipulation—it's about mastering the art of human connection through preparation, empathy, and strategic action.

CHAPTER 2

The Three Lives of Your Customer

"

Every customer has three lives—public, private, and secret. Uncovering the hidden layers unlocks their true motivations.

"

Every customer you encounter has three lives: public, private, and secret. Understanding these layers is the key to unlocking their true motivations and crafting a sales approach that resonates. Much like an intelligence officer peeling back layers to understand a target, a salesperson must skillfully navigate these dimensions to understand what a client truly needs.

This chapter explores these three lives in detail, offering techniques for identifying and connecting with each layer, and showing how doing so can lead to deeper trust and greater success in your sales efforts.

The Three Lives Defined

1. Public Life

This is the version of themselves your customer willingly shows to the world. It includes their job title, LinkedIn profile, company affiliations, and the polished, professional persona they project. The public life is where most sales conversations start, as this is the surface-level information readily available to you.

Example:

A client's public life might reveal they are the "Director of Operations at a manufacturing firm." They attend industry conferences and post regularly about supply chain efficiency on social media.

2. Private Life

The private life represents the thoughts, concerns, and goals your customer shares only with close colleagues or friends. This might include their frustrations at work, professional aspirations, or even concerns about their job performance. To access this layer, you must build rapport and demonstrate empathy.

Example:

Through casual conversation, you learn that the same Director of Operations is struggling to reduce downtime on production lines and is under pressure from leadership to meet tighter deadlines.

3. Secret Life

The secret life is the innermost layer, containing fears, desires, or insecurities that clients rarely share with anyone. This could be a fear of losing their job, a desire for recognition, or a deeply personal motivation driving their decisions. Accessing this layer requires a high degree of trust and sensitivity.

Example:

Over time, you discover that the Director of Operations isn't just worried about production downtime—they are afraid that if the next quarter's metrics don't improve, their leadership role might be at risk.

How to Uncover
the Three Lives

Step 1: Research the Public Life

Before meeting with a client, research their public persona:

- Review their LinkedIn profile and other social media accounts.

- Analyze their company's press releases, annual reports, or website.

- Look for any articles, interviews, or blogs they've contributed to.

Tip: Use this information to tailor your initial approach. Reference their public achievements or insights to build rapport.

Step 2: Listen for the Private Life

Once you engage with the client, listen closely for clues about their private life:

- Ask open-ended questions about their challenges and goals.
- Pay attention to tone and non-verbal cues when discussing sensitive topics.
- Build trust by sharing relatable experiences or expressing empathy.

Tip: Use phrases like, *"What's the biggest challenge you're facing this quarter?"* to prompt deeper insights.

Step 3: Build Trust to Access the Secret Life

The secret life requires time and trust. Focus on building a genuine relationship:

- Follow up consistently to show reliability.
- Offer value without expecting immediate returns (e.g., insights, tools, or introductions).
- Be discreet and respectful—never push too hard for personal information.

Tip: Frame questions around their professional goals, which often tie to personal motivations, such as, *"What would success look like for you personally if we solve this issue?"*

Why the Three Lives Matter in Sales

Understanding these layers allows you to align your pitch with what truly matters to the client. By addressing concerns and aspirations at deeper levels, you move from being just a salesperson to a trusted advisor.

Case Study: Aligning with the Three Lives

A software company was pitching its analytics tool to a potential client, the head of marketing at a mid-sized e-commerce business.

- From public research, the sales team knew the client was focused on increasing online conversions.

- During the meeting, they uncovered a private concern: the client was struggling to analyze customer data effectively due to outdated systems.

- As trust developed, the client revealed a secret fear: if conversion rates didn't improve soon, they worried their boss might replace them.

By addressing all three layers—public metrics, private challenges, and secret fears—the sales team positioned their software as not only a tool for better analytics but also as a career-saving solution. They closed the deal and gained a loyal client.

Workshop
Activities

Activity 1: Research and Present
1. Choose a partner and pretend they are a potential client.
2. Research their "public life" based on a provided LinkedIn profile or mock company background.

3. Present a tailored introduction pitch based on your findings.

4. Discuss feedback and refine your approach.

Activity 2: Role-Playing for Rapport

1. Break into groups of three: salesperson, client, and observer.

2. The salesperson asks open-ended questions to uncover the client's "private life" motivations.

3. The observer notes effective techniques and missed opportunities.

4. Rotate roles and debrief as a group.

Activity 3: Trust-Building Through Empathy

1. Create scenarios where clients share surface-level challenges but hide deeper fears.

2. Participants practice active listening and empathetic questioning to uncover the client's "secret life."

3. Discuss how to integrate these insights into a sales strategy.

By mastering the concept of the three lives, you'll develop a deeper understanding of your customers' motivations and learn to craft pitches that resonate on every level. This ability to connect and empathize will set you apart as a sales tactician who delivers not just products but solutions that truly matter.

Conclusion

Understanding that every customer has a public, private, and secret life gives you a unique advantage in sales. While most salespeople only engage with what's on the surface, true professionals dig deeper by building trust and uncovering unspoken motivations. The more effectively you can identify what truly drives your prospects, the better equipped you'll be to position your solution as the perfect fit for their needs— both the obvious and the hidden.

CHAPTER 3

Reading People Like a Spy

The unspoken speaks volumes—master the art of decoding body language and microexpressions to uncover what words can't convey.

Intelligence officers are experts in observing human behavior, decoding the subtle cues that reveal what someone is truly thinking or feeling. In sales, these same skills can help you uncover unspoken needs, identify objections before they're voiced, and adapt your approach in real time. By learning how to read microexpressions, body language, and behavioral patterns, you can develop a powerful advantage in your sales interactions.

This chapter explores these techniques and provides actionable steps to integrate them into your sales process.

The Importance of
Non-Verbal Communication

While words convey the message, non-verbal cues reveal the emotion behind it. Decoding these signals allows you to:

- Gauge a prospect's interest level.

- Identify hidden objections or resistance.

- Build rapport by responding to emotional cues.

Example:

Imagine you're presenting a solution to a client. They smile and nod (verbal agreement), but their arms are crossed, and their body is angled slightly away from you. These non-verbal signals suggest they might be feeling defensive or uncertain despite their polite words.

Microexpressions:
The Face Tells All

Microexpressions are involuntary facial expressions that last for only a fraction of a second. They can reveal a person's true emotions, even if they're trying to conceal them.

Common Microexpressions and Their Meanings

- **Happiness:** A genuine smile involves the eyes (crow's feet) as well as the mouth. A fake smile does not.

- **Disgust**: A wrinkled nose and raised upper lip.

- **Surprise:** Raised eyebrows, wide eyes, and an open mouth.

- **Anger:** Lowered eyebrows, tightened lips, or flared nostrils.

- **Fear:** Raised eyebrows, wide eyes, and slightly parted lips.

Example:

During a sales pitch, a client might say, *"That sounds interesting,"* but show a microexpression of disgust. This split-second reaction reveals they don't like what they're hearing. Noticing this allows you to pivot the conversation and address their concerns.

Body Language:
Speaking Without Words

Body language provides additional context to microexpressions and verbal communication. Pay attention to the following:

Positive Cues

- Open posture (uncrossed arms and legs).
- Leaning slightly forward (engagement and interest).
- Nodding (agreement or understanding).

Negative Cues

- Crossed arms (defensiveness or discomfort).
- Leaning away (disinterest or disengagement).
- Fidgeting (nervousness or impatience).

Example:

A prospect leans back and crosses their arms as you discuss pricing. These signals suggest resistance. Acknowledge their hesitation by saying, *"I sense you might have concerns about the cost—would you like to discuss that further?"*

Behavioral Patterns:
Connecting the Dots

Behavioral patterns are habits or recurring actions that reveal a prospect's decision-making style. Observing these patterns over time can help you tailor your approach.

Key Patterns to Observe

- **Verbal Choices:** Do they focus on risk avoidance or opportunities?

- **Pacing:** Are they quick decision-makers or deliberate planners?

- **Focus Areas:** Do they ask more about details or big-picture outcomes?

Example:

A client who repeatedly asks about case studies and ROI metrics likely prioritizes risk minimization. Frame your pitch to emphasize reliability and measurable results.

Bringing It All Together: A Sales Scenario

During a meeting, you notice the following:

1. The client maintains direct eye contact and nods during your introduction **(positive engagement)**.
2. When you mention implementation timelines, they frown briefly **(microexpression of concern)**.
3. Their fingers tap the table during your product demo **(impatience)**.

By decoding these cues, you realize they're interested but worried about delays. You pivot to emphasize your company's track record of on-time delivery, addressing their concern proactively.

Practical Tips for Reading People

1. **Practice Observation:** Start by watching people in everyday settings to identify microexpressions and body language.
2. **Stay Present:** Focus on your client's behavior in the moment, rather than planning your next statement.
3. **Look for Clusters:** Don't rely on a single cue; look for a combination of signals to confirm an insight.
4. **Adapt Your Approach:** Use what you observe to guide the tone, pace, and focus of your conversation.

Workshop

Activities

Activity 1: Microexpression Practice

1. Watch short video clips or use microexpression training tools online.

2. Identify the fleeting emotions displayed in each clip.

3. Discuss how these emotions might affect a sales conversation and brainstorm appropriate responses.

Activity 2: Body Language Role-Playing

1. Pair up with a partner. One person plays the client, displaying various body language cues (e.g., crossed arms, leaning forward).

2. The other person practices identifying the cues and responding appropriately.

3. Rotate roles and provide feedback on observations.

Activity 3: Behavioral Pattern Mapping

1. Choose a real or hypothetical client and list their known behaviors (e.g., frequent questions about risk, preference for data).

2. Discuss as a group how these patterns can guide your sales strategy.

3. Role-play tailoring a pitch based on these observations.

By mastering the art of reading people, you can anticipate needs, address concerns, and build stronger connections. Like a skilled operative, you'll approach every interaction with heightened awareness and precision, transforming how you connect with clients and close deals.

Conclusion

The ability to read people is one of the most powerful skills in sales. It's not just about hearing what someone says—it's about interpreting what they really mean through body language, tone, and microexpressions. By sharpening your observational skills and learning to decode the subtle signals that people reveal, you'll gain a deeper understanding of your prospects' emotions, needs, and concerns, allowing you to respond with tailored, effective solutions.

CHAPTER 4

Building Instant Rapport

"

Trust isn't built in days; it's built in moments—find common ground, mirror behavior, and demonstrate empathy.

"

In sales, the first few moments of any interaction are critical. Building rapport isn't just about being likable; it's about creating a connection that fosters trust and makes your client feel understood. Like Intelligence officers who must quickly establish trust with strangers in high-stakes situations, successful salespeople know how to form authentic bonds in a short amount of time. This chapter explores proven techniques— mirroring, finding common ground, and demonstrating empathy—that can help you build instant rapport with any client.

Why Rapport Matters

Rapport is the foundation of trust, and trust is the currency of influence. Without it, even the best pitch will fall flat. Clients who trust you are more likely to:

- Share their true needs and concerns.

- Be open to your solutions.

- Build a long-term professional relationship with you.

Example:

A financial advisor meets a new client who seems hesitant to discuss their goals. By mirroring their calm tone and emphasizing shared values like financial security for family, the advisor creates a sense of understanding, leading the client to open up about their retirement concerns.

Techniques for Building

Instant Rapport

1. Mirroring: The Subtle Art of Synchrony

Mirroring involves subtly mimicking the body language, tone, and pace of your client's speech. This technique creates a subconscious sense of familiarity and alignment.

How to Mirror:

- **Body Language:** If your client leans forward, lean forward slightly. If they use hand gestures, use them too—but naturally.

- **Tone and Pace:** Match their volume and speed. For instance, if they speak slowly and thoughtfully, avoid speaking too quickly.

- **Vocabulary:** Use similar terms or phrases. If they refer to "cost savings," mirror their language instead of using "budget reduction."

Example:

A tech salesperson notices a potential client frequently uses the phrase *"seamless integration."* In their pitch, the salesperson mirrors this language, saying, *"Our product ensures seamless integration with your current systems,"* creating alignment and trust.

2. Finding Common Ground

Common ground builds connections by highlighting shared interests, experiences, or goals. It shows your client that you understand their world.

How to Find Common Ground:

- **Do Your Research:** Look for mutual interests on LinkedIn, in past conversations, or through their company's content.

- **Listen Actively:** Pay attention to subtle clues they drop during conversations about hobbies, industry challenges, or personal values.

- **Ask Open-Ended Questions:** Questions like, *"What drew you to this role?"* or *"What's been the most exciting project you've worked on recently?"* can reveal shared experiences.

Example:

A salesperson pitching to a CEO mentions they both attended the same industry conference the previous year. This shared experience helps break the ice and opens the door for a more personal, engaging conversation.

3. Demonstrating Empathy

Empathy involves understanding and validating your client's feelings and perspectives. It's one of the fastest ways to build trust.

How to Demonstrate Empathy:

- **Acknowledge Their Concerns:** Repeat back what they've said to show you're listening (e.g., "I hear that delivery timelines are a big priority for you right now.").

- **Ask How They Feel:** Questions like, *"How do you feel about this approach?"* show you care about their perspective.

- **Offer Reassurance:** Provide solutions that address their concerns, but only after truly understanding them.

Example:

A client expresses frustration about previous vendors overpromising and underdelivering. Instead of jumping to a solution, the salesperson empathizes by saying, "I can see why that would be frustrating. Let's talk about how we ensure transparency and reliability in our process."

Bringing the Techniques Together

A real estate agent meets a young couple looking for their first home. The agent:

1. Mirrors their excitement and casual tone by leaning forward and smiling as they talk about their dream home.

2. Finds common ground by mentioning their own experience of buying a first home and the emotions that came with it.

3. Demonstrates empathy when they express anxiety about financing, saying, *"It's completely normal to feel this way. Let me walk you through the options step by step so it feels more manageable."*

Within minutes, the couple feels comfortable and trusts the agent to guide them through the process.

Workshop

Activities

Activity 1: Mirroring in Action

1. Pair up with a partner. One person plays the client, and the other plays the salesperson.

2. The "client" speaks for 2-3 minutes about a work challenge. The "salesperson" practices mirroring their body language, tone, and pace.

3. Afterward, the client gives feedback on how natural the mirroring felt.

Activity 2: Finding Common Ground

1. Break into small groups. Each participant shares one personal or professional interest.

2. Other participants ask questions to uncover shared interests or experiences.

3. Discuss how these discoveries could be used to build rapport in a sales setting.

Activity 3: Empathy Statements

1. Create a list of common client concerns (e.g., *"This solution feels risky for my team"*).

2. Practice responding empathetically with validation and reassurance (e.g., *"I understand why this feels risky. Let's explore how we can minimize that for you."*).

3. Role-play these scenarios in pairs and share feedback.

By mastering the art of building instant rapport, you can turn first impressions into lasting connections. Rapport paves the way for trust, and trust opens the door to deeper conversations, greater understanding, and more successful outcomes in sales. Like a skilled tactician, you'll approach every interaction with the tools to connect quickly and meaningfully.

Conclusion

Rapport is the bridge between interest and trust. In sales, building rapport isn't about small talk–it's about creating genuine human connections through empathy, mirroring, and shared experiences. When prospects feel understood and valued, they're more likely to engage with your solution. By practicing the techniques of active listening and personalized engagement, you can form relationships that go beyond transactions and lead to long-term success.

CHAPTER 5

The Psychology of Connection

"

People buy from those they like and trust—leverage reciprocity, authority, and likability to forge lasting relationships.

"

Deep, lasting relationships in sales aren't built on product features or price points—they're rooted in psychology. Understanding how people form connections, whom they trust, and what motivates them to act can transform how you approach every prospect. In this chapter, we'll explore three key psychological principles—*reciprocity, likability, and authority*—and how they can be leveraged to build trust, strengthen relationships, and drive results.

1. Reciprocity:

The Power of Giving First

Humans are wired to respond to generosity with generosity. This is the principle of reciprocity: when someone gives us something of value, we feel compelled to give something in return. In sales, offering value upfront creates goodwill and makes prospects more likely to engage, trust, and eventually buy from you.

How to Use Reciprocity in Sales

- **Offer Free Value:** Share insights, resources, or tools that align with your prospect's needs. For example:
  - » A market analysis report tailored to their industry.
  - » A free consultation or demo addressing their specific pain points.

- **Be Genuine:** Reciprocity only works when the gift feels sincere and not transactional.

- **Follow Through:** Consistently deliver on promises to build trust over time.

Example:
A software salesperson noticed a potential client's frustration with managing their data. Before pitching, the salesperson sent a free, customized dashboard template to help streamline the client's workflow. This act of generosity built goodwill, and the client later chose the salesperson's solution over a competitor's

2. Likability:

People Buy From Those They Like

It's a simple truth: we're more likely to trust and buy from people we like. Likability isn't about being overly charming–it's about being genuine, approachable, and relatable.

How to Cultivate Likability

- **Be Authentic:** People can spot insincerity a mile away. Speak honestly and avoid overpromising.

- **Show Interest:** Listen actively and ask thoughtful questions to show you care about their concerns and goals.

- **Find Common Ground:** Identify shared interests or experiences to create a bond.

Example:

A B2B salesperson noticed their prospect's LinkedIn profile mentioned a love of hiking. During their next conversation, the salesperson casually mentioned their recent hiking trip, leading to an enthusiastic exchange about favorite trails. This personal connection built trust and rapport, paving the way for a successful deal.

3. Authority:

Credibility Builds Confidence

We tend to trust experts and authority figures. By positioning yourself as a knowledgeable, credible resource, you can inspire confidence in your prospects and increase their likelihood of following your recommendations.

How to Establish Authority

- **Demonstrate Expertise:** Share case studies, industry insights, or success stories that highlight your knowledge.

- **Use Social Proof:** Highlight endorsements, testimonials, or partnerships with other respected companies.

- **Be Transparent:** Admit when you don't have an answer, and follow up with the right information. Honesty enhances your credibility.

Example:

A cybersecurity consultant won over a skeptical prospect by sharing a case study about how their solution mitigated a similar company's security breach. The consultant's expertise and transparency about the challenges made them the trusted choice.

Combining the Principles for Maximum Impact

These three principles—reciprocity, likability, and authority—are most powerful when used together. Imagine a scenario where:

- You offer a valuable insight **(reciprocity)**,
- Build a personal connection during the conversation **(likability)**,
- And back your solution with proven expertise and testimonials **(authority)**.

This approach creates a seamless, trust-driven relationship where prospects feel valued, understood, and confident in your ability to help them succeed.

Case Study: Putting It All Together

A marketing consultant was pitching their services to a mid-sized e-commerce business. Here's how they applied these principles:

1. **Reciprocity:** Before the meeting, they sent the prospect a free performance analysis of their website, highlighting areas for improvement.
2. **Likability:** During the meeting, they found common ground by discussing a shared passion for sustainable business practices.

3. **Authority:** They presented a portfolio of successful campaigns they had managed for similar businesses, including measurable results.

The combination of these elements created a strong connection, and the prospect chose the consultant over competitors who simply pitched their services without building a relationship.

Workshop
Activities

Activity 1: Practice Reciprocity
1. Break into small groups. Each participant shares a hypothetical prospect scenario.

2. Group members brainstorm what free value they could offer to build goodwill with the prospect (e.g., an article, template, or unique insight).

3. Share ideas and discuss how these acts of generosity might influence the prospect's perception.

Activity 2: Building Likability
1. Partner up and role-play a first meeting with a potential client.

2. Focus on asking questions to uncover shared interests or experiences. Practice responding authentically to build rapport.

3. Rotate roles and provide feedback on how natural and effective the likability-building techniques felt.

Activity 3: Establishing Authority

1. Choose a product or service you sell and list three ways to establish credibility (e.g., testimonials, case studies, personal expertise).

2. Role-play presenting your solution to a skeptical prospect, incorporating these credibility-building elements.

3. Group members critique how well authority was established and offer suggestions for improvement.

Conclusion

Understanding and leveraging the psychology of connection is a game-changer in sales. By giving value first (reciprocity), being relatable and genuine (likability), and establishing yourself as a credible expert (authority), you can forge stronger, trust-driven relationships with prospects. These principles are not just tools—they're the foundation for creating meaningful, lasting connections that drive success.

STRATEGIC PREPARATION

Success in sales doesn't happen by chance—it's the result of meticulous planning and preparation. Section 2, **Strategic Preparation**, equips you with the tools and techniques to approach every sales interaction like a well-planned mission. Drawing inspiration from spy agencies disciplined approach to intelligence gathering and execution, this section focuses on understanding your clients, anticipating challenges, and mapping out strategies to achieve your goals. In this section, you'll learn how to gather actionable insights, craft buyer profiles, and prepare contingency plans to ensure you stay ahead of the competition. By mastering strategic preparation, you'll enter every sales interaction with confidence, clarity, and the ability to adapt to any situation.

CHAPTER 6

Pre-Mission Planning for Sales

"

Every successful mission begins with preparation—research your prospect, map the journey, and plan for contingencies.

"

Intelligence officers never walk into a mission unprepared. They gather intelligence, anticipate potential challenges, and develop multiple strategies to ensure success. The same level of preparation can transform your sales process. Effective pre-mission planning allows you to anticipate your client's needs, address potential objections, and adapt to changing circumstances.

This chapter introduces intelligence officer style preparation techniques, including researching prospects, mapping out the sales journey, and planning contingencies to keep you ahead of the game.

Why Preparation Matters

Success in sales is rarely accidental. Planning equips you to:

- Approach each interaction with confidence.

- Tailor your pitch to your client's specific needs and motivations.

- Minimize surprises and setbacks by anticipating challenges.

Example:

A salesperson pitching a SaaS solution to a retail client researched the company's recent struggles with inventory management. By preparing a tailored proposal that directly addressed this issue, they secured the client's interest and built credibility as a problem-solver.

Step 1: Researching Prospects

Deep research is the foundation of effective sales preparation. Like an operative gathering intelligence, your goal is to uncover key insights that will inform your approach.

What to Research:

1. The Company:

- Review their website, annual reports, and press releases.

- Look for recent changes, such as mergers, expansions, or leadership shifts.

- Identify their goals and pain points based on industry trends.

2. The Individual:

- Study your prospect's LinkedIn profile to understand their role, experience, and interests.

- Check for mutual connections or shared interests.

- Look for clues about their decision-making style (e.g., detail-oriented vs. big-picture thinker).

3. The Market:

- Understand industry challenges and competitors.

- Be ready to explain how your solution addresses broader trends.

Example:

Before meeting with a healthcare client, a salesperson discovered the company's CEO had emphasized digital transformation in a recent interview. They tailored their pitch to highlight how their solution aligned with this priority.

Step 2: Mapping the Sales Journey

The sales journey is rarely linear. Mapping it out helps you anticipate each stage and guide your prospect smoothly toward a decision.

Key Stages to Map:

1. Initial Contact:

- What is the best way to approach this prospect (e.g., email, LinkedIn, referral)?

- What value can you offer immediately to grab their attention?

2. Needs Discovery:

- What questions will help you uncover their true needs?
- What objections or concerns are likely to arise?

3. Solution Presentation:

- How can you frame your product or service to align with their priorities?
- What case studies or data can you share to build credibility?

4. Closing:

- What signs will indicate they're ready to make a decision?
- How will you handle last-minute objections or hesitation?

Example:

A real estate agent created a step-by-step journey for a first-time homebuyer, starting with a checklist of financial documents to gather and ending with a timeline for closing. This clear roadmap made the process less intimidating and built trust.

Step 3: Preparing Contingencies

Even the best plans can encounter obstacles. Contingency planning ensures you're ready to adapt and keep the process moving forward.

Common Scenarios to Prepare For:

- **Budget Concerns:** Have alternative pricing options or discounts ready.

- **Technical Questions:** Bring a technical expert to the meeting or prepare detailed documentation.

- **Stakeholder Pushback:** Anticipate objections from other decision-makers and craft responses.

Example:

During a pitch to a logistics company, a salesperson faced unexpected resistance from the CFO about implementation costs. Because they had prepared an ROI analysis, they were able to demonstrate long-term cost savings, which addressed the concern and saved the deal.

Bringing It All Together: The Pre-Mission Checklist

Before every client interaction, ensure you've:

1. Researched
the company, the individual, and the market.

2. Mapped
out the stages of the sales journey.

3. Prepared
responses to potential objections or setbacks.

Case Study: Pre-Mission Planning in Action

A SaaS company was preparing to pitch its analytics platform to a large e-commerce retailer. The team:

- Researched the retailer's declining sales in specific regions (pain point).

- Mapped out a sales journey that began with a demo and ended with a tailored implementation plan.

- Prepared contingency plans for potential objections, including pricing concerns and integration challenges.

During the pitch, the retailer expressed concerns about the upfront cost. The team responded with data showing how the platform would boost regional sales, addressing the objection and closing the deal.

Workshop Activities

Activity 1: Prospect Research

1. Provide participants with a mock prospect profile (e.g., a company description and executive bio).

2. Have them research the company and individual using available resources (e.g., LinkedIn, press releases).

3. Each participant presents their findings and suggests how they would tailor their approach based on the research.

Activity 2: Sales Journey Mapping

1. Break participants into small groups and assign each group a mock sales scenario (e.g., pitching a new product to a CFO).

2. Groups map out the sales journey, identifying key stages, potential objections, and value propositions for each stage.

3. Each group shares their map and receives feedback.

Activity 3: Contingency Planning

1. Provide participants with a list of common sales objections (e.g., *"We don't have the budget for this right now."*).

2. In pairs, participants brainstorm responses or alternative strategies for each objection.

3. Role-play handling these objections during a mock sales pitch.

Conclusion

Pre-mission planning is your secret weapon for sales success. By researching your prospects thoroughly, mapping out the sales journey, and preparing for contingencies, you'll approach every interaction with confidence and clarity. Like an operative on a mission, you'll be ready for whatever comes your way, ensuring you stay one step ahead at every stage of the sales process.

CHAPTER 7

Open-Source Intelligence for Sales

---- " ----

Publicly available information is your secret weapon—use it to understand your prospect's world before the first conversation.

---- " ----

In the world of espionage, operatives often rely on open-source intelligence (OSINT)—publicly available information—to gather valuable insights about their targets. Similarly, in sales, leveraging OSINT can provide a competitive edge by helping you understand your prospects, their organizations, and their industries before you ever reach out. With this knowledge, you can tailor your approach, build rapport, and position your solutions effectively.

This chapter explores how to use publicly available data to learn about your prospects, their needs, and their challenges, enabling you to approach each sales opportunity like a well-informed tactician.

What is Open-Source Intelligence for Sales?

Open-source intelligence (OSINT) refers to information gathered from publicly accessible sources such as:

- Company websites
- Social media platforms
- News articles
- Industry reports
- Public financial filings

When applied to sales, OSINT allows you to:

1. **Understand** your prospect's role, priorities, and challenges.

2. **Identify** company goals, pain points, and market positioning.

3. **Tailor** your pitch to align with their specific needs and circumstances.

Example:

A salesperson researching a prospect discovers a recent press release announcing a company expansion into a new region. Armed with this information, they tailor their pitch to highlight how their product can support seamless scaling during this growth phase.

Sources of Open-Source Intelligence

1. Company Websites

- Review the company's *"About Us," "News,"* and *"Careers"* sections to understand their mission, goals, and recent developments.

- Look for product launches, partnerships, or strategic initiatives.

Example:

A SaaS company found a prospect's job posting for a "Data Analytics Specialist," indicating the company was investing in analytics capabilities. They framed their pitch around improving data-driven decision-making.

2. Social Media

- **LinkedIn:** Study your prospect's profile to learn about their role, career path, and professional interests. Look for shared connections or posts that reveal priorities.

- **Twitter:** Check for company announcements, leadership tweets, or industry opinions.

- **Instagram/Facebook:** Some companies share their culture or behind-the-scenes content, offering clues about their values and priorities.

Example:

A salesperson noticed a LinkedIn post from a prospect about sustainability. During their meeting, the salesperson highlighted how their solution reduced waste, aligning their pitch with the prospect's values.

3. News and Press Releases

- Use tools like Google News or industry publications to find recent news about the company or its leadership.
- Look for awards, financial results, or public statements.

Example:

An industrial supplier discovered a news article about a prospect securing a government contract. Knowing the project's scope, the supplier positioned their solution as ideal for meeting the project's requirements.

4. Industry Reports and Trade Publications

- Review market analysis, competitor comparisons, and industry trends to understand the broader context of your prospect's challenges.
- Use insights to show your expertise and position your solution as the best fit.

Example:

A medical equipment salesperson used an industry report highlighting regulatory changes to demonstrate how their product ensured compliance, gaining the trust of a hospital administrator.

5. Public Financial Filings

- For publicly traded companies, analyze quarterly earnings reports, annual reports, and investor presentations.
- Identify financial goals, risks, and areas of focus.

Example:

A B2B vendor noticed a prospect's annual report emphasized cutting operational costs. During the pitch, they highlighted how their solution reduced overhead and improved efficiency.

How to Use Open-Source Intelligence in Sales

1. Create a Prospect Profile

Compile key information about the individual and their organization:

- Job role and responsibilities.
- Company goals and pain points.
- Recent achievements or challenges.

2. Identify Conversation Starters

Use your findings to open the conversation with relevant insights. For example:

- *"I noticed your company recently launched a new product line—how has that been going?"*
- *"I saw your recent post about improving team productivity. I'd love to share how our tool can help."*

3. Tailor Your Pitch

Align your solution with the prospect's goals, challenges, or values based on the information you've gathered. This demonstrates that you understand their world and have come prepared to help.

Case Study:
OSINT in Action

A marketing agency was preparing to pitch their services to a mid-sized tech firm. Here's how they used OSINT:

1. **Company Website:** Found a press release announcing the company's goal to expand its digital presence.
2. **LinkedIn:** Learned that the marketing director had recently joined the company, likely indicating a fresh approach to strategy.
3. **Industry Reports:** Discovered that competitors in the same space were heavily investing in SEO and content marketing.

During the meeting, the agency tailored their pitch to focus on boosting the company's digital visibility and provided examples of how they had helped other tech firms achieve similar goals. The marketing director was impressed by their preparation and awarded them the contract.

Workshop
Activities

Activity 1: Prospect Research Challenge

1. Assign participants a mock prospect (e.g., a company name and job title).

2. Give them 15 minutes to research the company and individual using online sources (e.g., LinkedIn, Google News).

3. Have participants present their findings and suggest how they would tailor their sales approach based on the information.

Activity 2: Role-Playing with OSINT

1. Pair participants into groups of two. One plays the prospect and shares mock details about their company or challenges.

2. The other plays the salesperson and uses open-ended questions to uncover additional details, referencing their OSINT findings to guide the conversation.

3. Rotate roles and discuss the effectiveness of the approach.

Activity 3: Building a Prospect Profile

1. Provide participants with a blank prospect profile template, including sections for:
   - Job role and responsibilities.
   - Company goals and challenges.
   - Recent news or achievements.

2. Assign each participant a real or mock company to research.

3. Have them complete the profile and discuss how they would use this information in a sales pitch.

Conclusion

Open-source intelligence is one of the most powerful tools in your sales toolkit. By leveraging publicly available information, you can gain deep insights into your prospects' needs, goals, and challenges. With this knowledge, you'll approach every conversation with confidence, precision, and relevance, setting yourself apart as a salesperson who truly understands and delivers.

CHAPTER 8

The Buyer's Profile

"

The more you know your buyer, the better you can serve them—analyze motivations, decision-making styles, and pain points.

"

Understanding your buyer is the foundation of effective selling. Just as an intelligence officer develops a detailed dossier on their target, sales professionals can benefit from building comprehensive buyer personas. These profiles help you tailor your approach by identifying the motivations, decision-making styles, and pain points of your clients. When you truly understand what drives your buyer, you can speak directly to their needs and position your solution as the perfect fit.

In this chapter, you'll learn how to create detailed buyer profiles, leverage those profiles to enhance your sales strategy, and uncover actionable insights to close deals faster and with greater confidence.

What is a Buyer's Profile?

A buyer's profile is a detailed representation of your ideal client, based on research and data. It goes beyond surface-level information like job title or industry and digs into:

1. **Motivations:** What do they want to achieve?

2. **Decision-Making Style:** How do they process information and make choices?

3. **Pain Points:** What challenges are they trying to solve?

Example:

For a CFO, a buyer's profile might reveal that their primary motivation is cost reduction, their decision-making style is data-driven, and their pain point is managing operational inefficiencies.

Step 1: Analyze Motivations

Understanding what drives your buyer is key to aligning your solution with their goals. Motivations can be professional, personal, or a mix of both.

Common Motivations:

- **Growth:** Expanding market share, launching new products, or scaling operations.

- **Efficiency:** Saving time, reducing costs, or improving processes.

- **Recognition:** Gaining acknowledgment from peers or superiors.

Example:

A marketing manager's motivation might be to deliver a successful campaign that earns praise from their CEO. Highlighting how your solution can streamline campaign execution aligns directly with their goal.

How to Identify Motivations:

- **Ask open-ended questions** like, *"What does success look like for you?"*
- **Observe language cues** in conversations or emails (e.g., repeated focus on growth or risk mitigation).

Step 2: Understand
Decision-Making Styles

Not all buyers approach decisions the same way. Recognizing their decision-making style allows you to present information in a way that resonates.

Common Decision-Making Styles:

1. **Analytical:** Prefers data, detailed comparisons, and logical reasoning.

   Tip: Provide case studies, ROI analyses, and clear metrics.

2. **Emotional:** Driven by intuition, feelings, or alignment with values.

   Tip: Use storytelling and paint a vision of success.

3. **Consensus-Based:** Relies on input from a team or

other stakeholders.

Tip: Equip them with materials to share and build support internally.

4. **Decisive:** Focuses on speed and simplicity.

Tip: Present clear, actionable steps and avoid overloading with details.

Example:

A VP of Sales might be a decisive decision-maker. Rather than presenting a 30-slide deck, focus on the top three benefits of your solution and how quickly they can implement it.

Step 3: Pinpoint Pain Points

Pain points are the specific challenges or frustrations your buyer is trying to overcome. Addressing these directly can make your pitch irresistible.

Common Pain Points:

- **Operational:** Inefficiencies, delays, or resource constraints.
- **Financial:** Budget overruns or lack of ROI from existing solutions.
- **Strategic:** Falling behind competitors or failing to meet goals.

Example:

An IT director might be struggling with outdated infrastructure that causes frequent outages. Tailor your pitch to emphasize how your solution minimizes downtime and improves reliability.

How to Identify Pain Points:

- Listen carefully to what they emphasize in conversations.
- Research common challenges in their industry or role.
- Ask probing questions like, *"What's holding you back from achieving your goals?"*

Creating the Buyer's Profile

Key Elements to Include:

1. **Demographics:** Job title, industry, and company size.
2. **Motivations:** What drives them professionally and personally?
3. **Decision-Making Style:** How do they process information and make choices?
4. **Pain Points:** What challenges are they facing?
5. **Preferred Communication Style:** Do they prefer in-person meetings, email updates, or quick phone calls?

Example Profile:

- **Name:** Sarah Johnson
- **Role:** Director of Operations at a mid-sized manufacturing firm
- **Motivations:** Reduce production costs and streamline supply chain management

- **Decision-Making Style:** Analytical, prefers data-backed solutions

- **Pain Points:** High downtime on production lines, difficulty forecasting demand

- **Preferred Communication Style:** Detailed reports and email follow-ups

Using Buyer Profiles in Sales

1. Tailor Your Approach:

Use the profile to decide how to structure your pitch and what to emphasize.

2. Anticipate Objections:

Knowing their pain points and decision style helps you prepare for pushback.

3. Build Trust:

Demonstrating a deep understanding of their world shows you're invested in their success.

Example:

A salesperson pitching to Sarah Johnson (above) might focus on presenting case studies that demonstrate cost reductions and include data visualizations that highlight ROI.

Workshop

Activities

Activity 1: Build a Buyer's Profile

1. Provide participants with a mock client scenario (e.g., a CFO at a healthcare company).

2. Ask them to research the role and industry, then fill out a buyer's profile template with:
   - Motivations
   - Decision-making style
   - Pain points

3. Discuss how they would tailor their pitch based on the profile.

Activity 2: Decision-Making Role-Play

1. Pair participants. One acts as the buyer, the other as the salesperson.

2. The buyer adopts a specific decision-making style (e.g., analytical or emotional).

3. The salesperson tailors their pitch accordingly.

4. Rotate roles and provide feedback.

Activity 3: Uncovering Pain Points

1. Provide participants with a list of open-ended questions designed to uncover pain points.

2. In groups, participants practice asking these questions and responding to hypothetical answers.

3. Discuss the most effective questions and approaches.

Conclusion

Building a buyer's profile is like creating a map to navigate the sales process. By understanding your client's motivations, decision-making style, and pain points, you'll be equipped to deliver tailored solutions that resonate deeply. This level of preparation not only increases your chances of success but also positions you as a trusted partner who truly understands your client's needs.

GATHERING INTELLIGENCE

The ability to gather and interpret intelligence is what separates good salespeople from exceptional ones. In Section 3, **Gathering Intelligence**, you'll learn to uncover critical insights that help you tailor your approach, address hidden concerns, and deliver solutions that resonate deeply with your prospects. Inspired by the techniques used by Intelligence officers, this section focuses on turning every conversation, question, and observation into actionable intelligence. This section explores how to extract information subtly, interpret both verbal and non-verbal cues, and build a clearer picture of your prospect's needs and motivations. By mastering these skills, you'll be able to anticipate objections, adapt dynamically, and guide conversations with precision.

CHAPTER 9

The Art of Asking Questions

"

Great questions lead to great insights—ask open-ended, layered, and hypothetical questions to uncover the truth.

"

In sales, success often hinges on the quality of the questions you ask. Much like an operative gathering intelligence, a skilled salesperson knows how to ask the right questions to uncover deeper insights and motivations. The art of questioning isn't about interrogation—it's about creating a conversation that leads to understanding and connection.

This chapter explores adaptive questioning techniques, including open-ended, hypothetical, and layered questioning. You'll learn how to use these methods to reveal your prospect's true needs, address unspoken objections, and position your solution effectively.

Why Asking Questions is Crucial

Great questions serve multiple purposes in sales:

1. **Uncovering Needs:** By encouraging prospects to share their challenges and goals, you can tailor your pitch to meet their specific needs.

2. **Building Rapport:** Thoughtful questions show that you're genuinely interested in their perspective, fostering trust and connection.

3. **Guiding the Conversation:** Questions allow you to steer the conversation toward areas where your solution can provide value.

Example:

A salesperson asked a prospective client, "What's the biggest hurdle your team faces when meeting quarterly goals?" This open-ended question revealed a critical pain point—delayed reporting systems—allowing the salesperson to focus their pitch on solving this issue.

Types of Adaptive Questions

1. Open-Ended Questions

Open-ended questions encourage detailed responses, making them ideal for uncovering needs and building rapport. These questions begin with words like "what," "how," or "why" and invite the prospect to elaborate.

Examples:

- *"What are your top priorities for this quarter?"*
- *"How does your team currently handle this challenge?"*
- *"Why is this particular goal important to your company?"*

When to Use:

Start with open-ended questions early in the conversation to gather broad insights.

2. Hypothetical Questions

Hypothetical questions help prospects envision potential scenarios or outcomes. These questions are particularly effective for exploring possibilities and framing your solution.

Examples:

- *"If you could solve this problem instantly, what would success look like?"*
- *"How would your workflow improve if this process was automated?"*
- *"What would happen if your team could reduce downtime by 20%?"*

When to Use:

Use hypothetical questions to shift the conversation toward solutions and encourage creative thinking.

3. Layered Questions

Layered questions build on the prospect's previous answers, allowing you to dig deeper into their motivations and concerns. This technique shows you're actively listening and helps uncover the root of the issue.

Examples:

- **Prospect:** *"We're struggling to stay within budget."*

  Follow-up: *"What's causing the budget overruns?"*

  Further: *"How do these overruns affect your other projects?"*

- **Prospect:** *"Our team finds the current tool difficult to use."*

  Follow-up: *"What specific challenges are they facing with the tool?"*

  Further: *"How has that impacted productivity or morale?"*

When to Use:

Layered questions are effective when you want to clarify vague responses or explore deeper issues.

Framing Questions to Build Trust

The way you phrase your questions can either build trust or create resistance. Here are some tips:

- **Be Curious, Not Interrogative:** Ask questions in a conversational tone.

- **Show Empathy:** Use phrases like, *"I can imagine that must be challenging. Can you tell me more?"*

- **Avoid Leading Questions:** Instead of, *"Wouldn't you agree this is the best option?"* ask, *"What's your perspective on this approach?"*

Example:

A salesperson framed their question empathetically: *"I noticed your recent posts about team collaboration. What's been working well, and where do you see room for improvement?"* The prospect opened up about specific pain points, leading to a productive conversation.

Using Questions to Handle Objections

Strategic questions can turn objections into opportunities for deeper understanding:

- **Objection:** *"Your product seems too expensive."*

  Question: *"What's your budget for this project, and how do you prioritize features versus cost?"*

- **Objection:** *"We're happy with our current provider."*

  Question: *"What do you value most about their service, and are there areas where you'd like to see improvement?"*

Case Study: Questions Driving Success

A salesperson pitching a project management tool asked the following sequence:

1. **Open-Ended:** "What challenges are your teams facing with project deadlines?"

2. **Layered:** "Why do you think delays are occurring?"

3. **Hypothetical:** "How would having a centralized dashboard change that process?"

These questions revealed that the company's current tool lacked cross-team visibility, which led to missed deadlines. By addressing this specific pain point, the salesperson successfully closed the deal.

Workshop Activities

Activity 1: Open-Ended Question Practice

1. Split participants into pairs. One plays the prospect, the other the salesperson.

2. The salesperson practices asking open-ended questions to uncover the prospect's needs.

3. Rotate roles and provide feedback on the effectiveness of the questions.

Activity 2: Hypothetical Scenario Role-Play

1. Provide participants with a mock sales scenario and prospect profile.

2. Participants craft and ask hypothetical questions designed to explore solutions.

3. Group members discuss how the questions shifted the prospect's perspective.

Activity 3: Layered Questioning Drill

1. Present participants with a vague prospect statement (e.g., "Our team is struggling with communication.").

2. Participants practice asking layered follow-up questions to uncover deeper issues.

3. Share and critique the most effective follow-up strategies.

Conclusion

The art of asking questions is one of the most powerful tools in a salesperson's arsenal. By mastering adaptive techniques like open-ended, hypothetical, and layered questioning, you can uncover your prospect's true needs, guide conversations with confidence, and build trust along the way. As you hone your questioning skills, you'll transform every interaction into a meaningful dialogue that paves the way for success.

CHAPTER 10

Active Listening: Hearing What's Not Said

> *Listen not just to words but to tone, pauses, and omissions—they reveal hidden priorities and concerns.*

Sales isn't just about talking—it's about listening. But active listening goes beyond hearing the words your prospect says. It involves picking up on subtle cues like tone changes, key phrases, and even what's left unsaid. These clues often reveal hidden priorities, concerns, or objections that may not surface otherwise.

This chapter explores how to master active listening, helping you recognize and respond to the deeper layers of communication. With this skill, you'll build stronger relationships, address concerns proactively, and position your solution as the best fit.

What is Active Listening?

Active listening is a communication skill that requires full attention and engagement. It's about:

1. **Hearing the Words:** Absorbing what your prospect explicitly says.

2. **Reading Between the Lines:** Picking up on tone, hesitations, and omissions.

3. **Responding Thoughtfully:** Showing you've understood their message and probing deeper when needed.

Example:

A prospect says, *"We've tried similar tools before, and they didn't work."* Active listening identifies the hesitation in their tone and the use of "similar tools" as an opportunity to ask, *"What challenges did you face with those tools, and how did they fall short of expectations?"*

The Components
of Active Listening

1. Recognizing Key Phrases

Certain words or phrases can indicate priorities, objections, or hidden needs. Pay attention to:

- **Priority Indicators:** Words like *"must-have," "critical,"* or *"essential"* signal key decision factors.

- **Objection Indicators:** Phrases like *"we've tried this before"* or *"that seems expensive"* suggest concerns.

- **Exploration Cues:** Questions like *"How does this compare to X?"* or *"What happens if we don't use this?"* reveal where they need more clarity.

Example:

A prospect says, *"Our leadership team is focused on scalability this year."* The key phrase *"focused on scalability"* highlights a priority that you can address directly in your pitch.

2. Detecting Tone Changes

The way something is said often carries more weight than the words themselves. Listen for:

- **Excitement:** A raised tone or quicker pace can signal interest or enthusiasm.

- **Hesitation:** Pauses or a softer tone may indicate uncertainty or doubt.

- **Frustration:** A sharper tone might reveal underlying concerns or dissatisfaction.

Example:

While discussing pricing, a client's tone shifts from open to hesitant. Recognizing this change, you might say, "It seems like cost might be a concern. Would you like to discuss flexible payment options?"

3. Noticing Omissions

What isn't said can be just as telling as what is. If a prospect avoids discussing certain topics, it may indicate discomfort or lack of confidence.

Example:

If a decision-maker avoids mentioning other stakeholders, it might suggest internal disagreements. Address this by asking, "Who else might be involved in making this decision?"

Techniques to Enhance
Active Listening

1. Paraphrasing and Clarifying

Rephrasing what the prospect has said shows you're listening and ensures mutual understanding.

Example: *"So what I'm hearing is that reducing downtime is your top priority—did I get that right?"*

2. Non-Verbal Engagement

Use body language to show attentiveness:

- Maintain eye contact.
- Nod subtly to encourage them to continue.
- Avoid distractions like looking at your phone.

3. Strategic Pausing

Allow moments of silence after they've spoken. This encourages them to elaborate and can reveal deeper insights.

Example:

After a prospect says, *"We're exploring a few different options,"* wait a moment before responding. They may continue with, *"But we're leaning toward a solution that integrates easily with our current systems."*

Active Listening in Practice

Scenario 1: Priorities Revealed

During a discovery call, a prospect says, *"Our team is really stretched thin right now."* Recognizing the frustration in their tone, you ask, *"What kind of support would help lighten the load?"* This opens the door to positioning your solution as a time-saver.

Scenario 2: Objections Uncovered

A client says, *"We're not sure if this is the right time for a change."* By picking up on their hesitancy, you respond, *"What concerns you most about making a change now?"* This reveals specific objections you can address.

Scenario 3: Hidden Stakeholders

A prospect repeatedly says, *"I think this will work for us,"* but avoids mentioning their boss or team. You ask, *"Who else will be involved in finalizing this decision?"* This uncovers additional stakeholders you need to engage.

Workshop

Activities

Activity 1: Recognizing Key Phrases

1. Provide participants with sample prospect statements (e.g., "We've had issues with implementation in the past.").

2. Have them identify key phrases and discuss how they'd respond.

3. Share insights as a group.

Activity 2: Tone Change Scenarios

1. Role-play a conversation where the prospect's tone changes during the discussion (e.g., enthusiasm shifts to hesitation when pricing is mentioned).

2. Participants practice identifying and responding to the change.

3. Rotate roles and provide feedback.

Activity 3: The Power of Silence

1. In pairs, one participant plays the prospect and gives brief, vague answers (e.g., "We're considering a few options.").

2. The other participant practices pausing strategically after each answer to encourage elaboration.

3. Discuss how effective silence can lead to deeper insights.

Conclusion

Active listening is more than just a skill—it's a mindset. By recognizing key phrases, tone changes, and omissions, you'll uncover the deeper motivations and concerns that drive your prospects. This level of attentiveness not only builds trust but also positions you as a partner who truly understands their needs. As you hone your ability to hear what's not said, you'll gain the insights needed to navigate conversations with precision and confidence.

CHAPTER 11

Elicitation 101

—————— **" "** ——————

The best insights are freely given—create an environment where prospects feel safe sharing valuable information.

—————— **" "** ——————

Elicitation is the art of subtly and naturally extracting information during a conversation. Used masterfully by Intelligence officers, this technique involves asking the right questions and guiding discussions to uncover critical details—often without the other person even realizing they're sharing valuable insights. In sales, elicitation helps you uncover hidden needs, concerns, and motivations, all while building trust and making the prospect feel at ease.

In this chapter, you'll learn how to use conversational techniques to extract information effectively. By incorporating these skills into your sales interactions, you'll gain deeper insights into your prospects and position yourself as an attentive and trustworthy partner.

What is Elicitation in Sales?

Elicitation is a conversational strategy that encourages people to share information freely, without feeling interrogated. It involves:

1. **Building Comfort:** Creating a relaxed, non-threatening atmosphere.

2. **Guiding the Conversation:** Asking questions or making statements that prompt the prospect to share details.

3. **Listening Actively:** Using subtle cues to follow up and dig deeper.

Example:

Instead of directly asking, *"What's your company's budget?"* you might say, *"I've seen companies in your industry allocate around X% of their budget to this. Does that align with your experience?"* This approach makes the question feel conversational and invites the prospect to share their perspective.

Elicitation Techniques

1. THE ASSUMPTION TECHNIQUE

Make a statement that assumes knowledge or a common scenario, prompting the prospect to correct or elaborate.

How It Works:

- **Statement:** "I imagine that onboarding new hires must be a major challenge for your team."

- **Response:** The prospect might confirm, elaborate, or correct: "Actually, it's not onboarding but training that's the bigger issue."

Why It Works:

People naturally want to clarify or provide additional information when an assumption is made.

2. THE FLATTERY TECHNIQUE

Compliment the prospect on their expertise or achievements to encourage them to share more.

How It Works:

- **Statement:** "It seems like your team has done an excellent job optimizing your workflow. How did you achieve that?"

- **Response:** The prospect may share specific strategies or challenges they faced, revealing valuable insights.

Why It Works:

People are more likely to open up when they feel respected and recognized.

3. THE OPEN-ENDED QUESTION

Use broad, open-ended questions to invite the prospect to share their thoughts and feelings.

How It Works:

- **Question:** "What has been the most challenging aspect of scaling your operations?"

- **Response:** The prospect provides a detailed answer, highlighting pain points or priorities.

Why It Works:

Open-ended questions remove the pressure of a yes/no response, leading to richer conversations.

4. THE CURIOSITY TECHNIQUE

Express genuine curiosity about their role, processes, or challenges to draw them into a conversation.

How It Works:

- **Statement:** *"I've always been curious about how companies like yours approach sustainability goals. What's your strategy?"*

- **Response:** The prospect shares their approach, providing insight into their values and priorities.

Why It Works:

Curiosity disarms prospects by framing the conversation as a learning opportunity rather than a sales pitch.

5. THE HYPOTHETICAL SCENARIO

Pose a "what if" question to explore possibilities and reveal priorities.

How It Works:

- **Question:** "If you could solve one major challenge in your supply chain today, what would it be?"

- **Response:** The prospect shares their top concern, which you can then address.

Why It Works:

Hypotheticals encourage prospects to think creatively and share insights they might not reveal otherwise.

Practical Tips for Elicitation

1. **Stay Conversational:** Keep your tone natural and relaxed to avoid making the prospect feel like they're being interrogated.

2. **Follow the Breadcrumbs:** Pay attention to what they say and use follow-up questions to dive deeper.

3. **Respect Boundaries:** If the prospect hesitates or deflects, shift the focus to another topic to maintain trust.

4. **Balance Listening and Talking:** Let the prospect do most of the talking while you guide the conversation subtly.

Elicitation in Action

SCENARIO 1: Uncovering Pain Points

Prospect: *"We've been dealing with some workflow bottlenecks."*

You: *"I see that a lot with companies in your industry. Is it more about internal processes or external vendor delays?"*

Result: The prospect elaborates, revealing a key pain point with external vendors that you can address.

SCENARIO 2: Learning About Decision-Making

You: *"I've noticed companies your size often involve multiple departments in decisions like this. How do decisions typically get made at your company?"*

Prospect: *"We usually involve the CFO and the operations manager."*

Result: You now know the key stakeholders you need to engage.

SCENARIO 3: Exploring Budget Constraints

You: *"Many companies I've worked with allocate 10-15% of their budget to improving customer experience. Does that sound about right for your team?"*

Prospect: *"Actually, we've been working with a smaller budget this year—closer to 8%."*

Result: You gain insight into their financial limitations, allowing you to adjust your proposal accordingly.

Workshop
Activities

Activity 1: Role-Playing Elicitation Techniques

1. Pair participants and assign one as the salesperson and the other as the prospect.

2. The salesperson practices using elicitation techniques (e.g., assumption, flattery, curiosity) to gather information about the prospect's challenges or goals.

3. Rotate roles and provide feedback on how effectively the techniques were applied.

Activity 2: The "Hidden Insight" Game

1. Provide participants with mock prospect profiles that include hidden motivations or concerns (e.g., "The CFO is focused on cutting costs, but the operations manager wants scalability.").

2. Participants use elicitation techniques to uncover the hidden insights.

3. Discuss which techniques were most effective and why.

Activity 3: Crafting Elicitation Questions

1. Divide participants into groups and assign them a specific scenario (e.g., pitching to a marketing director at a mid-sized firm).

2. Each group creates a list of elicitation questions tailored to the scenario.

3. Groups present their questions, and the facilitator provides feedback on their effectiveness.

Conclusion

Elicitation is a subtle yet powerful tool for uncovering the insights you need to close deals. By mastering techniques like assumptions, flattery, and open-ended questions, you'll be able to gather information naturally and build trust along the way. With practice, elicitation will become an integral part of your sales conversations, setting you apart as a tactician who listens, learns, and delivers precisely what the client needs.

CHAPTER 12

Deception Detection

> *Inconsistencies in language, tone, and behavior are the breadcrumbs to uncovering hidden agendas.*

In sales, it's not uncommon for prospects to withhold information, exaggerate, or even mislead you about their intentions. Whether they're avoiding commitment, hiding objections, or playing vendors against each other, being able to detect deception is a critical skill. Like Intelligence officers trained to identify dishonesty, sales professionals can benefit from analyzing inconsistencies in language, tone, and body language to uncover the truth and navigate conversations effectively.

In this chapter, you'll learn how to recognize signs of dishonesty or hidden agendas and how to respond in a way that keeps the relationship intact while guiding the conversation toward clarity.

Why Detecting Deception Matters

Understanding when someone isn't being truthful can help you:

1. **Uncover Hidden Objections:** Address concernsv prospects might be hesitant to share.

2. **Avoid Wasting Time:** Identify prospects who aren't serious about moving forward.

3. **Build Credibility:** Show prospects you're perceptive and focused on solving real issues.

Example:

A prospect claims, "We're ready to make a decision next week," but avoids setting up a follow-up meeting. By identifying this discrepancy, you can probe further and uncover their hesitation, such as needing approval from additional stakeholders.

Common Signs of Deception

1. Verbal Cues

Deceptive language often includes subtle inconsistencies or patterns designed to obscure the truth. Look for:

- **Vague Statements:** Phrases like *"maybe," "possibly,"* or *"we'll see"* signal uncertainty.

- **Overly Formal Language:** Using unnecessarily complex

or rehearsed language may indicate a lack of authenticity.

- **Contradictions:** Inconsistent details or changes in the narrative are red flags.

Example:

Prospect: *"We've already allocated budget for this project."*

Later: *"We're still finalizing budget discussions."*

Response: *"You mentioned earlier that the budget was already allocated. Has something changed recently?"*

2. Tone and Speech Patterns

Changes in tone or speech patterns can reveal discomfort or dishonesty. Pay attention to:

- **Hesitation:** Long pauses or filler words like *"um"* or *"uh"* may indicate someone is thinking too hard about their response.

- **Overemphasis:** Statements like, *"I swear this is 100% true,"* often signal an attempt to convince rather than inform.

- **Inconsistencies in Volume or Speed:** A sudden change in how loudly or quickly someone speaks can indicate nervousness.

Example:

A prospect who was speaking confidently about their needs suddenly becomes quieter and hesitant when discussing timelines. This could signal reluctance to commit.

3. Body Language

Non-verbal cues can be some of the most telling signs of dishonesty. Watch for:

- **Avoiding Eye Contact:** While not always a sign of dishonesty, frequent avoidance of eye contact during critical moments can indicate discomfort.

- **Fidgeting:** Excessive movements, like tapping fingers or adjusting clothing, may signal nervousness.

- **Barriers:** Crossing arms, placing objects between themselves and you, or leaning away can suggest defensiveness.

Example:

During a pricing discussion, a prospect leans back and crosses their arms while saying, *"This fits perfectly within our budget."* This behavior may suggest they're hiding concerns about cost.

How to Respond to
Potential Deception

1. Stay Calm and Non-Confrontational

Accusing someone of dishonesty can damage trust. Instead, use curiosity and empathy to encourage them to share more.

Example:

"I get the sense that something might be holding you back. Could you help me understand what's on your mind?"

2. Ask Clarifying Questions

Probe gently to uncover inconsistencies without making the prospect defensive.

■ Example:

"You mentioned that timeline isn't an issue, but I noticed you hesitated earlier when we discussed deadlines. Is there something we should be mindful of?"

3. Focus on Building Trust

If you suspect dishonesty, reinforce your role as a partner rather than an adversary.

■ Example:

"I want to make sure we're addressing your real priorities here. If there's anything we haven't covered, I'd love to hear it."

Deception Detection in Action

SCENARIO 1: Budget Concerns

Prospect: *"This fits perfectly within our budget."*

You notice their tone becomes rushed, and they avoid eye contact.

Response: *"Budget is always an important factor. Are there any constraints I should be aware of to make sure we stay aligned?"*

SCENARIO 2: Stakeholder Involvement

Prospect: *"I'm the only decision-maker for this purchase."*

Later in the conversation, they mention needing feedback from their team.

Response: *"It sounds like your team plays an important role in decisions like this. How can we involve them in this process?"*

SCENARIO 3: Timeline Evasion

Prospect: *"We're planning to implement this immediately."*

Their body language shows hesitation, such as leaning back or fidgeting.

Response: *"That's great to hear! Can we map out the steps together to ensure everything is on track?"*

Workshop
Activities

Activity 1: Spotting Verbal Cues

1. Provide participants with scripted prospect statements that include deceptive cues (e.g., contradictions, vagueness).

2. Participants identify the red flags and suggest follow-up questions.

3. Discuss the most effective approaches as a group.

Activity 2: Role-Playing with Body Language

1. Pair participants and assign one as the prospect and the other as the salesperson.

2. The "prospect" incorporates subtle deceptive body language (e.g., fidgeting, leaning away) into their responses.

3. The salesperson practices identifying the cues and responding tactfully.

4. Rotate roles and provide feedback.

Activity 3: Tone and Inconsistency Exercise

1. Create a scenario where a prospect's tone or statements shift during the conversation.

2. Participants take turns practicing how to address these shifts with empathy and curiosity.

3. Discuss how tone and language inconsistencies can reveal hidden concerns.

Conclusion

Detecting deception isn't about "catching" your prospect in a lie—it's about understanding what's driving their behavior and addressing their real concerns. By analyzing inconsistencies in language, tone, and body language, you can uncover hidden priorities and objections while maintaining trust and rapport. With these skills, you'll navigate complex conversations with confidence, ensuring your solutions align with your prospect's true needs.

INFLUENCING DECISIONS

In sales, your ultimate goal is to guide prospects toward confident, informed decisions in favor of your solution. Section 4, **Influencing Decisions**, equips you with strategies and techniques to inspire action, overcome hesitation, and present your offering as the ideal choice. Drawing inspiration from psychological principles and intelligence methods, this section teaches you how to align your pitch with your prospect's needs and decision-making process. By mastering these skills, you'll position yourself as a trusted advisor who empowers prospects to act decisively.

CHAPTER 13

The Power of Framing

"

Control the narrative, and you control the decision—use framing, anchoring, and loss aversion to position your solution.

"

In sales, how you present your product or service can be just as important as what you're offering. The way you frame your pitch influences how your prospect perceives its value, relevance, and urgency. Drawing from psychological principles like *framing, anchoring*, and *loss aversion*, this chapter explores how to position your solution effectively to create maximum impact.

By mastering these techniques, you'll learn to guide your prospect's thinking, emphasize the benefits of taking action, and make your offer irresistible.

What is Framing?

Framing is the art of presenting information in a way that shapes how it is perceived. People don't make decisions in a vacuum; they interpret information based on context. The right frame can make a product seem more valuable, a price more reasonable, or a decision more urgent.

■ **Example:**

Instead of saying, *"Our solution costs $20,000 annually,"* you could frame it as, *"For just $1,667 per month, you can streamline your operations and increase productivity by 30%."* The second framing shifts the focus from cost to value.

Key Framing Techniques

1. Anchoring

Anchoring involves establishing a reference point that influences how your prospect evaluates subsequent options. The first number, idea, or concept introduced often sets the mental "anchor" for the conversation.

How to Use Anchoring:

- **Highlight the High-End Option First:** Present a premium offering first to make other options seem more reasonable.

■ **Example:** *"Our enterprise package is $50,000 annually, but most mid-sized businesses like yours find the $20,000 package to be the perfect fit."*

- **Compare Against a Larger Benchmark:** Contrast your price or solution against higher costs to create a sense of value.

Example: *"Our solution is a fraction of what you'd pay for a full-time employee to handle this manually."*

2. Loss Aversion

Loss aversion is the psychological principle that people are more motivated to avoid losses than to gain equivalent benefits. By framing your solution in terms of what your prospect stands to lose, you create urgency and drive action.

How to Use Loss Aversion:

- **Highlight Potential Risks of Inaction:** Emphasize the consequences of not addressing a problem.

Example: *"Without this system, your downtime could cost you $10,000 a day in lost revenue."*

- **Emphasize Missed Opportunities:** Frame benefits as something they might miss out on.

Example: *"By waiting, you could miss the chance to lock in this pricing before it increases next quarter."*

3. Benefit-Focused Framing

Shift the focus from the features of your product to the benefits it delivers, especially those aligned with the prospect's priorities.

How to Use Benefit-Focused Framing:

- **Translate Features into Outcomes:** Instead of saying, *"Our software has automated reporting,"* say, *"Our software saves your team 10 hours a week by automating reporting."*

- **Tie Benefits to Specific Goals:** Show how your solution helps them achieve what matters most.

- **Example:** "This tool will help you reduce customer churn by improving response times, directly supporting your retention goals."

Practical Applications
of Framing

SCENARIO 1: Anchoring in Price Conversations

When discussing pricing for a mid-tier software package:

- Start by mentioning the premium option at $50,000 to anchor the discussion.

- Present the $20,000 option as a great value in comparison.

- Frame it as, *"This package gives you 90% of the functionality of the premium plan for less than half the cost."*

SCENARIO 2: Loss Aversion for Urgency

A logistics company hesitates to upgrade their system despite inefficiencies.

- **Highlight losses:** *"Each day your trucks run at half capacity, you're leaving $5,000 in revenue on the table."*

- **Create urgency:** *"If we implement this now, you'll see savings by next quarter. Delaying could cost tens of thousands in missed opportunities."*

SCENARIO 3: Benefit-Focused Framing

When pitching a marketing solution:

Say, *"This platform improves your customer targeting by 25%, increasing your ROI on ad spend by an average of $15,000 annually,"* rather than, *"Our platform uses AI for better targeting."*

Framing Pitfalls to Avoid

1. **Overcomplicating the Frame:** Keep your message clear and focused. Too much information can dilute the impact.

2. **Using Fear Excessively:** While loss aversion is powerful, overusing fear-based framing can erode trust.

3. **Forgetting the Prospect's Priorities:** Always align your frame with what matters most to the client.

Workshop
Activities

Activity 1: Anchoring Practice

1. Provide participants with a product and two pricing tiers.

2. Have them craft an anchored pricing pitch, starting with the higher tier before introducing the lower one.

3. Present to the group and discuss the effectiveness of the anchors.

Activity 2: Loss Aversion Role-Play

1. Pair participants into salesperson and prospect roles.

2. The salesperson identifies a potential "loss" scenario for the prospect (e.g., lost revenue, inefficiency).

3. Practice framing the conversation around the risks of inaction. Rotate roles and provide feedback.

Activity 3: Benefit-Focused Reframing

1. Give participants a list of product features (e.g., "Automated workflows" or "Cloud-based storage").

2. Ask them to reframe each feature as a benefit tied to a specific prospect goal.

3. Share examples and discuss which reframing was most compelling.

Conclusion

Framing is a powerful tool for shaping how prospects perceive your product or service. By using anchoring to set benchmarks, leveraging loss aversion to create urgency, and emphasizing benefits to align with goals, you can guide your prospects toward seeing your solution as the best choice. With practice, these techniques will become second nature, helping you consistently position your offerings for maximum impact.

CHAPTER 14

Exploiting Cognitive Biases for Persuasion

> *Humans are wired to follow patterns—leverage biases like social proof, scarcity, and confirmation to influence decisions.*

Human decision-making is often influenced by subconscious mental shortcuts, known as cognitive biases. These biases affect how people perceive information, evaluate options, and make choices. By understanding and leveraging these biases, you can shape how prospects view your product or service and increase your ability to influence their decisions effectively.

In this chapter, we'll explore three powerful cognitive biases—confirmation bias, social proof, and scarcity—and how to use them to enhance your sales strategy. With practical examples and actionable techniques, you'll learn to turn psychological triggers into tools for persuasion.

What Are Cognitive Biases?

Cognitive biases are mental shortcuts people use to process information quickly. They often lead to predictable patterns of behavior, which can be leveraged to guide decision-making. In sales, these biases allow you to frame your pitch in ways that align with how people naturally think and act.

COGNITIVE BIAS 1: Confirmation Bias

Confirmation bias is the tendency for people to seek and interpret information that aligns with their existing beliefs. Once someone believes something, they naturally look for evidence to support that belief while discounting contradictory information.

How to Use Confirmation Bias:

1. **Reinforce What They Already Believe:** Position your solution as an extension of their current goals or values.

Example:

If a prospect values innovation, frame your product as *"the most cutting-edge solution in the market."*

2. **Validate Their Choices:** Acknowledge their past decisions and show how your offering complements those.

Example:

"Your decision to focus on customer retention has been a smart strategy. Our platform helps you build even deeper relationships with your customers."

COGNITIVE BIAS 2: Social Proof

Social proof is the phenomenon where people look to others' actions or opinions to determine their own. When prospects see others like them benefiting from your solution, they're more likely to trust and adopt it.

How to Use Social Proof:

1. **Highlight Testimonials and Case Studies:** Share success stories from similar clients or industries.

   Example: *"Companies like yours have seen a 25% increase in efficiency using our tool. Here's how one of them implemented it."*

2. **Emphasize Popularity:** Mention metrics that demonstrate widespread adoption.

   Example: *"Over 500 businesses trust us to streamline their operations."*

3. **Leverage Peer Influence:** Connect prospects with satisfied customers who can vouch for your product.

   Example: *"I'd be happy to introduce you to another marketing director who saw great results with our solution."*

COGNITIVE BIAS 3: Scarcity

Scarcity bias is the perception that limited availability makes something more valuable or desirable. When people believe they might miss out on an opportunity, they're more likely to act quickly.

How to Use Scarcity:

1. **Limit Time or Availability:** Create urgency by emphasizing deadlines or limited stock.

   - **Example:** *"We only have three spots left for implementation this quarter."*

2. **Highlight Exclusivity:** Make your offer feel special or unique.

   - **Example:** *"This pricing is only available to early adopters who sign up before the end of the month."*

3. **Frame Delayed Action as a Loss:** Show what they stand to lose by waiting.

   - **Example:** *"If we delay implementation, you might miss the opportunity to capitalize on the upcoming holiday sales season."*

Combining Cognitive
Biases in Sales

SCENARIO 1: The Power of Social Proof and Scarcity

A SaaS salesperson pitching to an e-commerce company highlights a case study (social proof) showing how a similar business increased their conversion rates. They add urgency by saying, *"We're only onboarding a limited number of clients before Black Friday, so we can dedicate resources to your success (scarcity)."*

SCENARIO 2: Confirmation Bias and Social Proof

When pitching to a CFO who values cost efficiency, a salesperson validates the prospect's existing focus: *"Your emphasis on reducing overhead aligns perfectly with our tool's ability to cut operational costs by 20%."* They then share a testimonial from another CFO who achieved similar results.

Practical Tips for Using
Cognitive Biases

1. **Be Authentic:** Overusing these techniques or fabricating urgency can backfire. Ensure your claims are genuine and supported by evidence.

2. **Know Your Audience:** Tailor your approach to the biases most likely to resonate with your prospect's personality and priorities.

3. **Use Biases to Empower Decisions:** Frame your pitch to help prospects feel confident and informed, rather than manipulated.

Workshop
Activities

Activity 1: Identifying Cognitive Biases

1. Provide participants with example sales scenarios and scripts.

2. Ask them to identify where confirmation bias, social proof, or scarcity are being used.

3. Discuss how effectively each bias was leveraged and suggest improvements.

Activity 2: Crafting Social Proof

1. Assign participants a mock product or service.

2. Have them write a testimonial, case study, or reference scenario that leverages social proof.

3. Share and critique the examples as a group.

Activity 3: Building Scarcity in Pitches

1. Provide participants with a product and a timeline (e.g., "Implementation slots are filling quickly").

2. Have them craft a pitch that incorporates scarcity to create urgency.

3. Practice delivering the pitch and provide feedback on its impact.

Conclusion

Cognitive biases are powerful tools for influencing decisions when used ethically and strategically. By leveraging confirmation bias, social proof, and scarcity, you can guide prospects toward seeing your solution as the clear choice. As you practice applying these psychological triggers, you'll gain the ability to craft persuasive pitches that resonate deeply and drive action.

CHAPTER 15

The Storytelling Advantage

> *Facts inform, but stories inspire—use compelling narratives to connect emotionally and reinforce logical value.*

Stories are how we make sense of the world. They connect us emotionally, help us visualize outcomes, and make information memorable. In sales, storytelling is a powerful tool to inspire trust, build rapport, and reinforce the value of your solution. A compelling narrative bridges the gap between logic and emotion, helping prospects see how your product or service fits into their story.

In this chapter, you'll learn how to craft and deliver stories that resonate with your audience, connect emotionally, and provide a logical foundation for decision-making. By blending facts with relatable narratives, you can transform your pitch into an engaging, persuasive experience.

Why Storytelling Works in Sales

Stories engage both the logical and emotional parts of the brain. While data appeals to logic, stories spark emotions and create a deeper connection. By combining the two, you make your pitch not only convincing but also memorable.

Example:

Instead of saying, *"Our software reduces project timelines by 30%,"* tell the story of a client who was able to launch a new product early because of your solution, beating competitors to market and exceeding revenue goals.

Elements of a Great Sales Story

1. The Hero (Your Prospect)

The best sales stories put the prospect at the center. They should see themselves as the hero who overcomes challenges with your solution as their guide.

How to Frame It:

- Describe a situation similar to theirs.
- Highlight how someone in their position succeeded using your product or service.

2. The Conflict (Their Challenge)

Every compelling story includes a challenge or problem. The more clearly you articulate this pain point, the more your prospect will identify with the story.

How to Frame It:

- Use specific examples that mirror their situation.

- Avoid overly generic challenges; make it relatable and tangible.

■ **Example:**

"They were spending so much time on manual data entry that critical insights were being missed. This led to slower decision-making and falling behind competitors."

3. The Resolution (Your Solution)

This is where your product or service comes in. Show how it solves the problem and delivers measurable results.

How to Frame It:

● Be specific about the benefits your solution provides.

● Use data or results to reinforce the story's credibility.

Example:

"By implementing our platform, they cut reporting time by 75%, giving them the ability to make data-driven decisions in real time. Within six months, they regained their competitive edge."

4. The Outcome (The Transformation)

End your story with a clear vision of success. Paint a picture of what life looks like after the problem is solved.

How to Frame It:

- Focus on the emotional and practical benefits.

- Show how your solution leads to long-term success.

Example:

"Today, their team operates more efficiently than ever, and they're on track to hit their growth targets for the third year in a row."

Story Formats for Sales

1. Success Stories

Highlight how a previous client achieved results using your product or service.

Example:

"Our tool helped a mid-sized retailer boost their e-commerce sales by 40% during the holiday season by automating their inventory updates."

2. Future Vision Stories

Help the prospect visualize success by projecting them into a future where their problem is solved.

Example:

"Imagine your team saving 20 hours a week on repetitive tasks. What would you accomplish with that extra time?"

3. Overcoming Objections

Use stories to address common concerns or objections.

Example:

"One of our clients was initially hesitant about the cost but soon realized the ROI far outweighed the investment. Within a year, they saw a 300% return."

Practical Tips for
Effective Storytelling

1. **Know Your Audience:** Tailor the story to their specific industry, role, and challenges.

2. **Be Concise:** Keep your stories focused and relevant. Avoid unnecessary details.

3. **Incorporate Data:** Blend emotional appeal with logical evidence to create a balanced narrative.

4. **Practice Delivery:** A well-delivered story is as important as the content itself. Use tone, pacing, and body language to enhance engagement.

Storytelling in Action

SCENARIO 1: Pitching to a Time-Strapped Manager

Instead of saying:
"Our software automates tasks to save you time,"

Try this:
"Last month, I worked with a project manager who felt overwhelmed by repetitive tasks. With our solution, she was able to free up her schedule to focus on strategic planning. Within two months, her team hit their goals ahead of schedule."

SCENARIO 2: Addressing Cost Concerns

Instead of saying:
"The investment is worth it,"

Try this:
"One of our clients, a CFO, had similar concerns about budget. After implementing our solution, they reduced operational costs by 20%, saving $50,000 annually."

Workshop

Activities

Activity 1: Build a Success Story

1. Assign participants a fictional product or service.
2. Ask them to craft a success story using the four key

elements: Hero, Conflict, Resolution, and Outcome.

3. Participants share their stories with the group, and the facilitator provides feedback.

Activity 2: Story Reframing

1. 1. 2. 3. Provide participants with a generic product benefit (e.g., "Our tool improves productivity").

2. Ask them to reframe it into a compelling story.

3. Discuss which reframes were most engaging and why.

Activity 3: Delivering Stories with Impact

1. Pair participants and have them practice delivering a story to their partner.

2. Partners provide feedback on tone, pacing, and emotional connection.

3. Rotate roles and repeat.

Conclusion

Storytelling is a powerful way to connect emotionally with your prospects while reinforcing the logical value of your solution. By crafting compelling narratives that put your prospect at the center, address their challenges, and showcase the transformation your product can deliver, you'll create memorable, persuasive pitches. With practice, storytelling will become one of your most effective tools for building trust, overcoming objections, and closing deals.

CHAPTER 16

Selling the Spy Way: Crafting Actionable Briefs

"

The clearest message wins—present insights that are concise, actionable, and tailored to your audience.

"

In spy agencies, intelligence operatives distill complex information into concise, actionable briefs designed to inform high-stakes decision-making. These briefs are clear, targeted, and focused on what matters most to their audience. In sales, adopting this approach allows you to deliver compelling insights tailored to your prospect's decision-making style, cutting through the noise and driving action.

This chapter teaches you how to craft actionable briefs that position your solution as the obvious choice. By focusing on clarity, relevance, and next steps, you'll ensure your presentations resonate and prompt decisive action.

The Importance of
Actionable Briefs

In today's fast-paced world, decision-makers are bombarded with information. A well-crafted brief:

1. **Saves Time:** Busy prospects value concise communication that gets to the point.
2. **Drives Clarity:** Highlights key points and removes unnecessary complexity.
3. **Guides Decisions:** Clearly defines the next steps, reducing hesitation or indecision.

Example:

Instead of presenting a lengthy report about your product's features, you create a one-page summary focusing

Key Components of
an Actionable Brief

1. Clear Objective

Define the purpose of your brief. What action do you want your audience to take? Every point in your brief should align with this objective.

Example Objective:

Convince a CFO to approve the budget for your software by demonstrating its ROI.

2. Tailored Insights

Focus on what matters most to your audience. Different stakeholders care about different things:

- **CFOs:** ROI, cost savings, financial impact.

- **CMOs:** Customer engagement, brand growth, lead generation.

- **CEOs:** Big-picture goals, market competitiveness, scalability.

Example:

For a CMO: *"Our platform increases customer engagement by 25%, helping you generate 30% more qualified leads per quarter."*

3. Supporting Evidence

Back up your insights with data, case studies, or testimonials. Be specific and relevant.

Example:

Case Study: *"XYZ Corp reduced operational costs by $50,000 annually using our solution, achieving ROI within six months."*

4. A Call to Action (CTA)

End with a clear, actionable step. Avoid leaving your audience wondering what to do next.

Example CTA:

"Let's schedule a 30-minute follow-up to finalize implementation details and set up your onboarding process."

Steps to Crafting
an Actionable Brief

STEP 1: Know Your Audience

Understand their priorities, pain points, and decision-making style. Tailor the tone and content accordingly.

Example:
If your audience values efficiency, emphasize time savings and streamlined implementation.

STEP 2: Focus on the Essentials

Resist the urge to overload your brief with details. Include only what is necessary to achieve your objective.

Example:
Instead of listing all 15 features of your product, highlight the top three that address the client's biggest challenges.

STEP 3: Use Visuals for Clarity

Graphs, charts, or bullet points make complex information easier to digest. Visuals also break up text, keeping your audience engaged.

Example:
A bar chart showing cost savings over time can be more persuasive than a paragraph of text.

STEP 4: Frame the Opportunity

Highlight the benefits of acting now and the risks of delaying.

■ Example:

"By implementing this solution this quarter, you'll be positioned to capitalize on the upcoming holiday season, driving an additional $200,000 in revenue."

STEP 5: End with Next Steps

Include a clear, specific action your prospect should take after reviewing the brief.

■ Example:

"Sign the proposal by Friday to lock in discounted pricing and secure onboarding by the end of the month."

Examples of Actionable Briefs

SCENARIO 1: Pitching to a CFO

- **Objective:** Secure budget approval for a new CRM.
- **Key Insights:**
  - » *"Current inefficiencies cost your team an estimated $5,000 per month."*
  - » *"Our CRM improves workflow efficiency, saving $60,000 annually."*
- **CTA:** *"Let's set up a 15-minute call to review ROI projections and finalize budget allocation."*

SCENARIO 2: Persuading a CMO

- **Objective:** Demonstrate how your platform enhances customer engagement.
- **Key Insights:**
  - » *"Our tool increases website engagement by 30% within three months."*
  - » *"Case Study: ABC Corp saw a 25% lift in lead conversions after implementation."*
- **CTA:** *"We can schedule a demo this week to show how the platform aligns with your goals."*

SCENARIO 3: Addressing a CEO's Big-Picture Goals

- **Objective:** Position your solution as a strategic advantage.
- **Key Insights:**
  - » *"Implementing this solution now positions your company to outpace competitors by improving scalability."*
  - » *"Projected market growth in your sector is 15% next year; our tool helps you capture that growth faster."*
- **CTA:** *"I'd like to present a detailed roadmap in a follow-up meeting next Wednesday."*

Workshop
Activities

Activity 1: Craft a Targeted Brief

1. Provide participants with a fictional prospect profile (e.g., CFO of a manufacturing company).

2. Ask them to craft a one-page actionable brief tailored to the prospect's priorities.

3. Present the briefs and discuss which were most effective and why.

Activity 2: Visualizing Data

1. Assign participants a product benefit (e.g., cost savings, increased efficiency).

2. Have them create a simple visual (e.g., chart, infographic) to support the benefit.

3. Share the visuals and discuss their impact.

Activity 3: Role-Playing Brief Delivery

1. Pair participants and assign one as the salesperson and the other as the prospect.

2. The salesperson delivers their actionable brief, focusing on clarity and relevance.

3. Partners provide feedback, emphasizing what worked and areas for improvement.

Conclusion

Crafting actionable briefs is a powerful way to distill complex information into clear, compelling insights that resonate with your audience. By tailoring your message, supporting it with evidence, and ending with a clear call to action, you'll ensure your prospects see the value in your solution and are motivated to act. With practice, you'll master the art of delivering briefs that drive results and build trust.

OPERATING IN COMPLEX ENVIRONMENTS

Sales is rarely straightforward, and success often depends on your ability to navigate complex environments. Section 5, **Operating in Complex Environments**, equips you with the skills and strategies to thrive in high-pressure situations, manage challenging conversations, and maintain control in multifaceted negotiations. Drawing inspiration from field operations, this section teaches you to adapt to shifting dynamics, neutralize resistance, and make calculated moves that lead to success. This section focuses on the practical techniques you need to handle hostility, manage competitive threats, and guide conversations with precision—even in the most challenging scenarios.

CHAPTER 17

Situational Awareness in Sales

> " "
>
> *The best salespeople read the room and adapt in real time—situational awareness turns shifting dynamics into opportunities.*
>
> " "

Situational awareness—the ability to perceive and respond to changing dynamics in real-time—is a skill that distinguishes exceptional salespeople from the rest. Like Intelligence officers who adapt to fluid circumstances in the field, successful sales professionals stay attuned to verbal and non-verbal cues, power shifts, and external factors during meetings or negotiations.

In this chapter, you'll learn how to cultivate situational awareness, adapt strategies as dynamics shift, and ensure you stay in control of the conversation. With real-world examples and actionable techniques, you'll develop the agility needed to navigate even the most complex sales interactions.

The Importance of Situational Awareness

Sales conversations and negotiations are rarely static. Situational awareness helps you:

1. **Read the Room:** Detect subtle changes in mood, engagement, or priorities.

2. **Adapt Your Approach:** Shift tactics based on new information or unexpected challenges.

3. **Maintain Control:** Keep the conversation aligned with your goals despite shifting dynamics.

Example:

During a negotiation, a prospect who was initially collaborative suddenly becomes defensive. Recognizing this shift, you adjust your tone and focus on rebuilding rapport before continuing the discussion.

Key Elements of Situational Awareness

1. Observing Non-Verbal Cues

Non-verbal signals often reveal more than words. Pay attention to:

- **Body Language:** Leaning in or away, crossed arms, or fidgeting.

- **Facial Expressions:** Smiles, furrowed brows, or raised eyebrows.

- **Eye Contact:** Maintaining or avoiding eye contact can signal engagement or discomfort.

> **Example:**
> If a decision-maker starts leaning back and crossing their arms, they may feel skeptical or disengaged. Address this by asking an open-ended question to re-engage them: *"Does this align with what you're looking for?"*

2. Listening for Verbal Shifts

Changes in tone, word choice, or pacing can signal a shift in the conversation.

- **Tone:** A shift from enthusiastic to hesitant may indicate doubt.

- **Pacing:** Faster speech may signal excitement, while slower responses may suggest caution.

- **Word Choice:** Repeated use of words like "concerned" or "unsure" may highlight objections.

> **Example:**
> If a prospect suddenly says, *"I'm not sure this is the right time,"* it may reflect a new concern. Probe gently: *"It sounds like timing might be a challenge. Can you share more about what's going on?"*

3. Monitoring Group Dynamics

In multi-stakeholder meetings, power dynamics and group interactions often influence decisions.

- **Who Holds Influence:** Identify who leads the conversation or whose opinion carries weight.

- **Engagement Levels:** Note who is actively participating versus who seems disengaged.

- **Alignment:** Look for signs of agreement or disagreement among stakeholders.

Example:

During a meeting, the CFO is quiet while the COO drives the discussion. By observing their body language, you notice the CFO nodding slightly when cost-saving benefits are mentioned. This signals they may support your solution but need to be drawn into the conversation.

4. Adjusting to External Factors

External factors like time constraints, interruptions, or unexpected challenges can shift dynamics.

- **Time Pressure:** If the meeting runs long, prioritize key points and propose a follow-up.

- **Interruptions:** Acknowledge and redirect focus to maintain momentum.

- **Competitor Mentions:** Stay calm and emphasize your unique value proposition.

Example:

If a prospect mentions a competitor's lower price, instead of reacting defensively, you highlight your differentiators: *"That's a great option for companies looking for basic functionality. We specialize in advanced capabilities that drive long-term value."*

Strategies for Enhancing Situational Awareness

1. Prepare for Flexibility

Anticipate potential shifts and plan contingencies. Ask yourself:

- What objections might arise?
- How can I redirect the conversation if engagement drops?
- Who are the key decision-makers, and how do I address their priorities?

2. Stay Present

Focus entirely on the conversation rather than thinking ahead to your next point. This allows you to pick up on subtle cues and adapt dynamically.

3. Use Clarifying Questions

When you sense a shift, use clarifying questions to uncover underlying concerns or motivations.

- *"Can you tell me more about that?"*
- *"How does this align with your goals?"*

4. Pause and Reflect

If you notice tension or resistance, pause briefly to collect your thoughts before responding. A thoughtful response is often more effective than an immediate reaction.

Situational Awareness in Action

SCENARIO 1: Detecting Skepticism

During a presentation, you notice a prospect frowning and leaning back. Instead of continuing with your pitch, you address their concern:

"I sense there might be something on your mind. What's your perspective on this so far?"

This approach opens the door for them to voice their concern, which you can then address directly.

SCENARIO 2: Navigating Group Dynamics

In a meeting with multiple stakeholders, one individual repeatedly interrupts others. Recognizing their influence, you acknowledge their input while ensuring others have a chance to speak:

"That's a great point. I'd love to hear how the rest of the team feels about this as well."

SCENARIO 3: Responding to Time Constraints

A prospect mentions they only have 15 minutes instead of the scheduled 30. You adapt by focusing on the most critical points and offering to follow up with additional details:

"Let's focus on the key benefits today, and I'll send you a detailed summary afterward."

Workshop

Activities

Activity 1: Non-Verbal Cue Observation

1. Pair participants and have one role-play as a prospect showing specific non-verbal cues (e.g., crossed arms, avoiding eye contact).

2. The other participant identifies the cues and adapts their approach accordingly.

3. Rotate roles and discuss how well the cues were identified and addressed.

Activity 2: Group Dynamics Role-Play

1. Create a scenario with multiple stakeholders, assigning roles with different priorities and engagement levels.

2. One participant acts as the salesperson, navigating the group dynamics to keep the meeting on track.

3. Discuss the strategies used and their effectiveness.

Activity 3: Adapting to Shifts

1. Provide participants with a mock sales meeting where the situation changes (e.g., new objections arise, a key stakeholder joins late).

2. Participants practice adapting their approach in real time.

3. Share feedback on how well they maintained control and advanced the conversation.

Conclusion

Situational awareness is a critical skill for staying in control of sales conversations and adapting to unexpected changes. By observing non-verbal cues, listening for shifts in tone, and responding to group dynamics, you'll build trust and keep discussions productive. With practice, you'll develop the agility to navigate any situation, ensuring your strategy remains aligned with your goals and your prospect's needs.

CHAPTER 18

Handling Hostility and Resistance

> *Conflict is a chance to connect—use tactical empathy to de-escalate tension and turn resistance into understanding.*

In sales, resistance is inevitable. Whether it's a skeptical prospect, a frustrated client, or a high-pressure negotiation, the ability to handle hostility with grace and effectiveness can turn challenging interactions into opportunities. Drawing from de-escalation techniques, this chapter introduces strategies like tactical empathy to defuse tension, rebuild trust, and steer the conversation toward a productive outcome.

By mastering these techniques, you'll learn to approach conflict with confidence, transforming moments of resistance into turning points for success.

Why Hostility and Resistance Happen in Sales

Hostility or resistance often arises due to:

1. **Misaligned Expectations:** The client's needs or assumptions don't align with your offering.

2. **Past Negative Experiences:** The prospect may have been let down by similar products or services.

3. **Pressure or Stress:** External factors, such as tight deadlines or budget constraints, can make prospects more defensive.

4. **Fear of Risk:** Concerns about making the wrong decision can lead to skepticism or hesitation.

Example:

A prospect frustrated by previous failed implementations may greet your pitch with resistance, even if your solution perfectly addresses their needs.

Key Techniques for Handling Hostility and Resistance

1. Tactical Empathy

Tactical empathy is the ability to recognize and articulate your prospect's emotions without judgment. It involves actively listening, acknowledging their feelings, and demonstrating understanding.

How to Use Tactical Empathy:

- **Acknowledge Their Perspective:** "I understand why you might feel frustrated given past experiences."

- **Validate Their Emotions:** "That sounds like a challenging situation. I'd feel the same way if I were in your position."

- **Avoid Defensiveness:** Focus on listening instead of immediately countering their objections.

Example:

If a prospect says, *"I've wasted time and money on solutions like this before,"* respond with tactical empathy: *"I hear you. It sounds like you've had some frustrating experiences. Let's discuss how we can ensure this works differently for you."*

2. De-Escalation Through Neutral Language

Hostile interactions can escalate if emotional language is mirrored. Neutral, calm responses help defuse tension.

Examples of Neutral Language:

- Instead of: *"That's not true,"* say, *"I see why it might feel that way."*

- Instead of: *"You're misunderstanding,"* say, *"Let me clarify what I mean."*

Example:

If a prospect says, *"Your product is way too expensive,"* respond calmly: *"I understand cost is an important factor. Let's explore how the value we provide aligns with your budget priorities."*

3. Focus on the Underlying Concern

Resistance often stems from an underlying concern that hasn't been articulated. Use open-ended questions to uncover the root cause.

Questions to Ask:

- *"What's the biggest challenge you see with this approach?"*
- *"Can you share more about what's driving your hesitation?"*

Example:

A client resists committing to a timeline, saying, *"This feels rushed."* By probing further, you learn they're concerned

4. Reframe the Conversation

Shift the focus from the conflict to shared goals or opportunities. This demonstrates that you're on the same side.

Reframing Techniques:

- **Highlight Shared Goals:** *"We both want to find the best solution for your team's needs."*
- **Emphasize Positive Outcomes:** *"If we can address this challenge, imagine the impact it could have on your business."*

Example:

If a prospect is resistant to adopting new technology, reframe by emphasizing benefits: *"I understand that change can feel risky. Let's talk about how this transition can actually make your team's work*

5. Take a Collaborative Approach

Inviting the prospect to contribute to the solution can reduce hostility and build trust.

Examples of Collaboration:

- *"What would an ideal solution look like for you?"*
- *"How can we adjust this approach to better meet your needs?"*

Example:

When a prospect criticizes a feature, respond collaboratively: *"Thank you for that feedback. How would you like to see this feature improved to better suit your process?"*

Turning Hostility
into Opportunity

When handled effectively, hostile interactions can strengthen relationships by demonstrating your ability to remain calm, empathetic, and solutions-focused.

Case Study:

A frustrated client was upset about delays in service delivery. Instead of getting defensive, the salesperson used tactical empathy:

"I completely understand why this delay is frustrating. Let's walk through what happened and make sure we address this moving forward."

The salesperson's calm and proactive approach not only resolved the issue but earned the client's loyalty.

Workshop

Activities

Activity 1: Tactical Empathy Role-Play

1. Pair participants. One plays a hostile prospect, while the other practices using tactical empathy to de-escalate.

2. Switch roles and provide feedback on tone, language, and effectiveness.

3. Discuss which empathetic statements worked best and why.

Activity 2: Uncovering Root Concerns

1. Present participants with a scenario where a prospect resists an idea (e.g., *"This solution feels risky"*).

2. Participants practice asking open-ended questions to uncover the root cause.

3. Share responses as a group and refine techniques.

Activity 3: Collaborative Problem-Solving

1. Assign groups a conflict scenario (e.g., a prospect objects to pricing).

2. Each group brainstorms a collaborative approach to resolve the issue.

Conclusion

Hostility and resistance are inevitable in sales, but they don't have to derail the conversation. By using tactical empathy, neutral language, and collaborative problem-solving, you can defuse tension and turn challenging interactions into opportunities for connection and trust-building. With practice, you'll gain the confidence to handle even the most difficult situations, ensuring productive outcomes and stronger relationships.

CHAPTER 19

Counterintelligence in Sales

"

Stay one step ahead—recognize competitor tactics and protect your position with strategic countermeasures.

"

In the competitive world of sales, protecting your position is just as important as advancing it. Just as spy agencies employs counterintelligence strategies to safeguard sensitive information and neutralize threats, sales professionals can use counterintelligence techniques to protect their strategies, counteract competitors, and secure client relationships.

This chapter explores how to identify and counter competitor tactics, safeguard proprietary information, and maintain a competitive edge. With actionable strategies and examples, you'll learn how to anticipate and neutralize threats to your success.

What is Counterintelligence in Sales?

Counterintelligence in sales involves protecting your position and strategy while identifying and neutralizing competitive threats. This includes:

1. **Detecting Competitor Tactics:** Understanding how competitors are positioning themselves and countering effectively.

2. **Securing Information:** Safeguarding proprietary details about your offering, pricing, and strategy.

3. **Strengthening Client Loyalty:** Building relationships that minimize the impact of competitor influence.

Example:

During a negotiation, a competitor attempts to undercut your pricing. By identifying their tactic and emphasizing your solution's superior value and ROI, you protect your position and secure the deal.

Key Counterintelligence Strategies

1. Identify Competitor Tactics

Competitors often employ specific strategies to win deals. Recognizing these tactics early allows you to prepare an effective response.

Common Competitor Tactics and How to Counter Them:

- **Undercutting Pricing:** Competitors may offer deep discounts to win the deal.

  Counter: Emphasize your solution's unique value and long-term ROI, rather than engaging in a price war.

  Example: *"While their initial price is lower, our solution saves you $50,000 annually through reduced downtime."*

- **Sowing Doubt:** Competitors may highlight perceived weaknesses in your product or company.

  Counter: Proactively address potential objections and provide data or testimonials that build credibility.

  Example: *"You may hear concerns about our implementation process. Let me share a case study showing how we delivered ahead of schedule for a similar client."*

- **Leveraging Relationships:** Competitors may use existing connections within the prospect's organization to gain influence.

  Counter: Build multiple relationships within the organization to avoid reliance on a single stakeholder.

  Example: *"I'd love to set up a conversation with your operations team to ensure this solution aligns with their needs as well."*

2. Secure Proprietary Information

Protecting sensitive details about your offering, pricing, and strategy is crucial to maintaining a competitive edge.

Tips for Securing Information:

- **Control Access:** Share sensitive information only with trusted stakeholders and only when necessary.

    Example: Provide detailed pricing models during final negotiations, not early in the sales process.

- **Use NDAs:** When appropriate, require non-disclosure agreements to protect proprietary insights shared during discussions.

- **Monitor Competitor Inquiries:** Be cautious if a competitor masquerades as a prospect or leverages third parties to gain insights.

    Example:
    A prospect repeatedly asks detailed questions about your product roadmap. To safeguard proprietary plans, respond by highlighting general future enhancements without disclosing specifics:

    "We're always innovating to improve efficiency. Let's focus on how our current solution aligns with your immediate needs."

3. Build Client Loyalty

Strong client relationships are the best defense against competitor influence. By positioning yourself as a trusted advisor, you make it harder for competitors to gain traction.

Ways to Strengthen Loyalty:

- **Deliver Exceptional Value:** Go beyond the sale by providing ongoing support, insights, and value.

- **Example:** *"After implementation, our team will conduct quarterly reviews to ensure you're maximizing ROI."*

- **Anticipate Future Needs:** Proactively address challenges before they arise, demonstrating long-term commitment.

- **Example:** *"Based on your growth projections, let's discuss scaling options for next year."*

- **Personalize the Experience:** Tailor your communication and solutions to their specific priorities and goals.

- **Example:** *"I customized this proposal to align with your goal of reducing operational costs by 20%."*

4. Monitor Competitive Activity

Staying informed about your competitors' moves allows you to anticipate their strategies and adjust accordingly.

Sources for Monitoring Competitors:

- **Public Channels:** Monitor competitors' websites, social media, and press releases for updates on offerings or partnerships.

- **Industry Networks:** Leverage industry events or mutual connections to gather insights.

- **Feedback from Prospects:** Listen carefully to what prospects mention about competitor pitches.

Example:

If a prospect mentions a competitor's new feature, you can respond by highlighting your solution's unique advantages:

"That's a great addition to their product. Our solution offers similar functionality but also integrates seamlessly with your current systems."

Turning Counterintelligence Into Opportunity

Counterintelligence isn't just about defense—it's also a proactive strategy to position your solution as the superior choice.

Case Study:

A prospect was considering a competitor due to lower pricing. By analyzing the competitor's offering, the salesperson highlighted hidden costs like limited customer support. They reframed their higher price as a better long-term investment, securing the deal.

Workshop Activities

Activity 1: Spot the Competitor Tactic

1. Provide participants with scenarios where competitors use tactics like undercutting or sowing doubt.

2. Participants identify the tactic and brainstorm ways to counter it effectively.

3. Discuss responses as a group and refine strategies.

Activity 2: Securing Sensitive Information

1. Role-play a scenario where a prospect asks for proprietary details (e.g., future product plans).

2. Participants practice balancing transparency with discretion.

3. Share feedback on how well they protected sensitive information while maintaining trust.

Activity 3: Competitive Analysis

1. Assign participants a fictional competitor and ask them to research its tactics, strengths, and weaknesses.

2. Each participant creates a plan to counter the competitor in a sales scenario.

3. Present plans and discuss which strategies were most effective.

Conclusion

Counterintelligence in sales is about protecting your position, anticipating competitor tactics, and securing client loyalty. By staying alert, safeguarding proprietary information, and positioning yourself as a trusted partner, you'll maintain a competitive edge in even the most challenging markets. With practice, you'll not only neutralize threats but also turn them into opportunities for success.

CHAPTER 20

Leveraging the Power of Silence

> ❝
>
> *Silence is a tool of influence—pause strategically to create space for reflection and guide conversations toward success.*
>
> ❞

In the fast-paced world of sales, silence can feel uncomfortable. However, when used strategically, silence is one of the most powerful tools in a salesperson's arsenal. Pauses create space for reflection, encourage openness, and subtly shift the dynamic of a conversation in your favor. Like a skilled tactician, mastering the art of silence allows you to emphasize key points, handle objections, and create a natural path to closing deals.

This chapter explores how to use silence intentionally to improve communication, build trust, and guide your prospects toward decisions.

Why Silence is Powerful

1. **Encourages Openness:** Silence often compels others to fill the void, prompting your prospect to share more information.

2. **Creates Reflection:** A well-timed pause allows your prospect to process what's been said, increasing the impact of your message.

3. **Signals Confidence:** Strategic silence demonstrates control and composure, positioning you as a calm, confident professional.

4. **Reduces Pressure:** Pausing shows respect for your prospect's decision-making process and avoids coming across as overly aggressive.

Example:

After presenting your price, pausing instead of immediately justifying or elaborating gives the prospect time to absorb the information and respond.

Techniques for Using Silence Strategically

1. The Pause After Key Points

After delivering an important statement, pausing allows the significance of your words to sink in. This technique can also emphasize your confidence in the value you're offering.

Example:

When presenting a value proposition:

*"Our solution increases efficiency by 25%, saving your team 10 hours a week." **(Pause.)***

This silence lets the prospect consider the impact of those savings before responding.

2. The "Silent Question"

Instead of filling the space after asking a question, remain silent and let the prospect answer. This technique often encourages deeper, more thoughtful responses.

Example:

You ask: *"What's the biggest challenge your team faces right now?" **(Pause.)***

Even if there's a moment of silence, wait. The prospect may elaborate in ways that reveal critical insights.

3. The Negotiation Pause

During negotiations, silence can shift the balance of power by prompting the other party to rethink or adjust their position.

Example:

Prospect: *"This price feels a bit high for us."*

You respond with a slight nod and silence.

This pause creates discomfort for the prospect, often leading them to elaborate, clarify, or even reconsider their position without you needing to say a word.

4. Silence to Handle Objections

When faced with an objection, pausing before responding shows you're thoughtfully considering their concern. It also gives them time to soften their stance or even retract their objection.

Example:

Prospect: *"I'm not sure this will work for our team."*
You pause, then calmly respond: *"What's your main concern about implementation?"*

5. Silence in Closing

After asking for the sale, resist the urge to speak first. Allow the prospect to process the decision and respond in their own time.

Example:

You say: *"Does this proposal meet your goals?"* **(Pause.)** The silence gives them space to make their decision without feeling pressured.

Common Pitfalls to Avoid

1. **Filling the Silence with Nervous Rambling:** Speaking too quickly or over-explaining can dilute your message and undermine your confidence.

2. **Using Silence in the Wrong Context:** Pausing too long during an unrelated or casual part of the conversation may feel awkward or forced.

3. **Interrupting the Silence Too Soon:** Trust the process— give the prospect time to think and respond.

The Science of Silence in Sales

Psychological studies show that silence creates a sense of urgency in conversations. People are naturally uncomfortable with prolonged silence and often fill it by sharing more information, clarifying their thoughts, or moving closer to a decision.

Practical Applications

SCENARIO 1: Presenting a Solution

- **Salesperson:** *"Our platform can cut your customer support response time by 50%, ensuring higher client satisfaction and retention. " **(Pause.)***
- **Prospect:** *"That's impressive. How quickly can we implement it?"*

SCENARIO 2: Handling Pricing Concerns

- **Prospect:** *"This feels like a big upfront cost."*
- **Salesperson:** (Pauses, nodding slightly.)
- **Prospect:** *"But I can see how the long-term savings could offset it."*

SCENARIO 3: Closing the Deal

- **Salesperson:** *"Are you ready to move forward with this plan?" **(Pause.)***
- **Prospect:** *"Yes, let's do it."*

Workshop

Activities

Activity 1: Practicing the Pause

1. Pair participants. One plays the salesperson, the other the prospect.

2. The salesperson practices delivering a value statement, followed by a deliberate pause.

3. Rotate roles and provide feedback on how the silence influenced the prospect's response.

Activity 2: Silent Objection Handling

1. Assign participants common objections (e.g., "Your price is too high").

2. The salesperson practices responding by pausing first, then addressing the objection calmly.

3. Discuss how the pause affected the tone and outcome of the interaction.

Activity 3: Role-Playing Negotiation Silence

1. Split participants into pairs for a mock negotiation.

2. The prospect raises concerns or counteroffers, and the salesperson uses pauses strategically to guide the conversation.

3. Rotate roles and analyze how silence shifted the negotiation dynamics.

Conclusion

The power of silence lies in its ability to create space for reflection, encourage openness, and demonstrate confidence. By mastering the strategic use of pauses, you'll build stronger connections with your prospects, address concerns effectively, and close deals with greater ease. Like a skilled tactician, your ability to leverage silence will become one of your most persuasive tools in the sales process.

CLOSING DEALS AND BUILDING RELATIONSHIPS

Closing a deal is more than a transaction—it's the culmination of trust, strategy, and value alignment. Section 6, **Closing Deals and Building Relationships**, equips you with the tools to not only finalize agreements effectively but also lay the foundation for lasting partnerships. Inspired by the intelligence officers approach to building long-term networks, this section emphasizes strategies that turn prospects into loyal clients and clients into advocates. This section focuses on closing with confidence, nurturing trust, and creating a framework for ongoing collaboration. You'll learn how to balance assertiveness with empathy, position yourself as a long-term partner, and ensure that every deal is a step toward a deeper relationship.

CHAPTER 21

Trust is the Currency

> *Trust is earned with transparency, ethical practices, and consistency—it's the currency of all successful relationships.*

In sales, trust is the foundation of every successful relationship. Prospects buy from people and companies they believe in. Trust can take weeks or months to build but only moments to lose. By prioritizing transparency, ethical practices, and consistency, you can establish long-lasting credibility that sets you apart in a crowded marketplace.

This chapter explores the principles of building and maintaining trust. You'll learn how to communicate openly, deliver on promises, and navigate difficult situations without compromising your integrity. With trust as your currency, you'll create relationships that lead not only to closed deals but also to repeat business and referrals.

The Importance of Trust in Sales

Trust impacts every stage of the sales process:

1. **Engagement:** Prospects are more likely to engage with someone they perceive as honest and reliable.

2. **Decision-Making:** Buyers feel confident choosing solutions from trustworthy sources.

3. **Retention:** Clients remain loyal to salespeople and organizations they trust, even in competitive markets.

Example:

A prospect skeptical of a marketing tool trusted the salesperson because they admitted upfront, *"Our platform isn't perfect for every use case, but here's where we excel."* This transparency set the stage for a productive, trust-based relationship.

How to Build and Maintain Trust

1. Be Transparent

Honesty and openness lay the groundwork for trust. Acknowledge limitations, provide accurate information, and avoid overselling.

How to Be Transparent:

- **Admit What You Don't Know:** If you don't have an answer, promise to find out and follow through.

  Example: *"I'm not sure about that feature. Let me confirm with our product team and get back to you."*

- **Set Realistic Expectations:** Be clear about what your product or service can and cannot do.

  Example: *"We can't guarantee results in the first month, but most clients see significant improvements by the end of the first quarter."*

2. Use Ethical Selling Practices

Ethical behavior ensures that trust is built on a solid foundation and protects your reputation over time.

Ethical Selling Practices:

- **Prioritize the Prospect's Needs:** Focus on providing solutions that genuinely address their challenges.

  Example: If a lower-priced option meets their needs better, recommend it instead of upselling unnecessarily.

- **Avoid Manipulative Tactics:** Never pressure or mislead prospects into making decisions.

  Example: Instead of saying, *"You must decide today to get this deal,"* say, *"This pricing is valid through the end of the month, so you have time to evaluate."*

3. Deliver on Promises

Consistency in your actions reinforces your credibility. Always do what you say you will, when you say you will.

Tips for Delivering on Promises:

- **Follow Through Quickly:** If you promise a follow-up, deliver it promptly.

  Example: *"I'll send you the ROI analysis by 3 p.m.,"* and ensure it's in their inbox on time.

- **Underpromise and Overdeliver:** Exceed expectations whenever possible.

  Example: If you estimate a timeline of three weeks, deliver in two.

4. Navigate Difficult Situations with Integrity

When things go wrong, how you respond matters more than the mistake itself. Taking accountability builds trust even in challenging circumstances.

How to Handle Challenges:

- **Acknowledge the Issue:** Be upfront about what went wrong.

  Example: *"We missed the deadline, and I take full responsibility for that."*

- **Propose Solutions:** Show your commitment to making things right.

> **Example:** *"Here's what we're doing to ensure this doesn't happen again, and we'll expedite the next steps to make up for lost time."*

Trust-Building in Action

SCENARIO 1: Transparent Communication

A salesperson pitching a software tool acknowledges that it's less robust than a competitor's for analytics but emphasizes its superior user interface and customer support. The prospect appreciates the honesty and chooses the tool for its ease of use.

SCENARIO 2: Ethical Selling

A client expresses interest in an add-on feature. The salesperson advises against it because it doesn't align with the client's goals, building long-term trust instead of chasing short-term revenue.

SCENARIO 3: Delivering on Promises

A prospect is promised a proposal by the end of the day. The salesperson sends it hours early, along with a personalized video explanation, exceeding expectations.

Workshop

Activities

Activity 1: Transparency in Action

1. Provide participants with a sales scenario where a product has a clear limitation (e.g., higher price, fewer features).

2. Ask them to craft a response that acknowledges the limitation while emphasizing the product's strengths.

3. Share and critique responses, focusing on clarity and tone.

Activity 2: Ethical Dilemmas Role-Play

1. Present participants with ethical challenges (e.g., a prospect asks for a feature you don't offer).

2. Participants role-play handling the situation while maintaining trust and ethical integrity.

3. Discuss the importance of honesty and how it impacts long-term relationships.

Activity 3: Trust Audit

1. Ask participants to reflect on their recent sales interactions and identify areas where trust could have been strengthened (e.g., missed follow-ups, vague promises).

2. Have them develop a plan to improve trust-building habits.

3. Share best practices as a group.

Conclusion

Trust is the currency of sales, and it compounds over time. By practicing transparency, ethical behavior, and consistency, you'll build relationships that withstand challenges and foster long-term loyalty. When prospects and clients trust you, they see you as more than a salesperson—they see you as a partner invested in their success. With trust as your foundation, you'll not only close deals but also create meaningful, enduring connections.

CHAPTER 22

Timing is Everything

"

Know when to push, when to pause, and when to wait—timing makes the difference between hesitation and commitment.

"

In sales, success often depends not just on what you say or offer, but when you say or offer it. Timing plays a critical role in influencing decisions, building rapport, and maintaining momentum. Knowing when to push forward, when to pull back, and how to use urgency without being overbearing is a skill that can transform your sales approach.

This chapter explores the art of timing in sales—when to advance the conversation, when to create urgency, and when to let the prospect breathe. You'll learn how to balance assertiveness with patience, ensuring your actions align with the prospect's decision-making pace and comfort level.

Why Timing Matters in Sales

1. **Aligns with Decision-Making Processes:** Timing ensures your actions match the prospect's readiness to move forward.

2. **Builds Trust:** Respecting a prospect's timeline shows that you value their priorities and comfort level.

3. **Maintains Momentum:** Acting too soon or too late can disrupt the sales process, but proper timing keeps things moving smoothly.

Example:

A prospect is excited about a demo but hesitant to commit immediately. Rather than pushing for a decision, the salesperson schedules a follow-up meeting to address remaining concerns, keeping the conversation alive without creating pressure.

Key Principles of Timing in Sales

1. Read the Prospect's Signals

Watch for verbal and non-verbal cues that indicate readiness, hesitation, or resistance.

Signals to Push Forward:

- The prospect says: *"This sounds great. What's the next step?"*
- They actively engage by asking detailed questions or discussing implementation.

Signals to Pull Back:

- They say: *"We need more time to think about this."*
- Their body language shows disengagement, such as avoiding eye contact or leaning away.

Example:
If a prospect begins asking about timelines and onboarding processes, they're signaling readiness. A well-timed response might be: *"It sounds like you're ready to explore how we can get started. Should we look at an implementation schedule?"*

2. Create Urgency Without Pressure

Urgency is a powerful motivator, but overly aggressive tactics can backfire. Instead, frame urgency around genuine benefits and deadlines.

How to Create Effective Urgency:

- **Tie it to Benefits:** Highlight how acting now delivers immediate value.

  Example: "By starting this quarter, you'll be able to see results before the next budgeting cycle."

- **Use Natural Deadlines:** Reference upcoming events or time-sensitive offers without forcing the issue.

  Example: "Our early-bird pricing ends Friday, and I'd love for you to take advantage of it."

3. Respect the Prospect's Pace

Pushing too hard can damage trust, while pulling back too

far can stall momentum. Strike a balance by guiding the conversation at a pace that feels comfortable for the prospect.

How to Respect Their Pace:

- **Follow Their Lead:** Match the prospect's level of engagement and urgency.

Example: *"Would you like to schedule a follow-up this week, or does next week work better for your timeline?"*

- **Check In Regularly:** Ask open-ended questions to ensure alignment.

Example: *"How are you feeling about the process so far? Is there anything you'd like to revisit before moving forward?"*

4. Time Your Follow-Ups Strategically

Effective follow-ups maintain momentum without feeling intrusive. Tailor the timing and frequency based on the stage of the sales process.

Follow-Up Timing Tips:

- **After a Demo or Presentation:** Send a follow-up within 24 hours to reinforce key points and address questions.

- **When They Request More Time:** Wait a few days before checking in, respecting their need for space.

Example: *"I wanted to follow up on our conversation earlier this week. Have you had a chance to review the proposal?"*

Practical Applications
of Timing

SCENARIO 1: Knowing When to Push

A prospect shows excitement during a demo but hesitates when discussing price. Instead of pushing for immediate closure, the salesperson shifts focus:

"Let's break down the ROI to see how this fits into your budget. Would you like to dive into the numbers together?"

SCENARIO 2: Pulling Back Gracefully

A prospect says they need to discuss internally before making a decision. The salesperson respects their timeline:

"That makes sense. How about I check in with you next Wednesday to answer any questions that come up after your discussion?"

SCENARIO 3: Creating Genuine Urgency

A prospect is interested but undecided. The salesperson highlights a natural deadline:

"This promotion ends on Friday, and I'd love for you to benefit from the discounted rate. Do you think you'll have a decision by then?"

Workshop

Activities

Activity 1: Recognizing Timing Signals

1. Provide participants with mock sales scenarios featuring prospect cues (e.g., *"We're excited, but we need time to align internally."*).

2. Ask participants to decide whether to push forward, pull back, or create urgency.

3. Discuss the reasoning behind their choices and how different timing might affect the outcome.

Activity 2: Crafting Urgency Statements

1. Assign participants a product or service with a natural deadline (e.g., early-bird pricing or end-of-quarter incentives).

2. Have them craft urgency statements that feel authentic and benefit-focused.

3. Share and critique the statements as a group.

Activity 3: Role-Playing Follow-Ups

1. Pair participants for role-playing exercises. One acts as the prospect, the other as the salesperson.

2. Prospects provide feedback on whether the follow-ups felt well-timed or too aggressive.

3. Rotate roles and refine approaches based on group discussion.

Conclusion

Timing is everything in sales. By learning to read signals, create urgency without pressure, and respect your prospect's pace, you'll foster trust and guide the sales process more effectively. Whether it's knowing when to push, when to pull back, or when to let silence do the work, mastering timing ensures you strike the right balance every time. With practice, this skill will help you close deals while building strong, lasting relationships with your clients.

CHAPTER 23

Retention as a Spycraft Skill

> *Closing the deal is just the beginning—anticipate needs, deliver value, and cultivate loyalty for long-term success.*

In sales, closing the deal is only the beginning. The real success lies in retention—cultivating long-term relationships that yield repeat business, referrals, and enduring loyalty. Much like an operative maintains relationships with trusted contacts over time, sales professionals can build and sustain meaningful connections by staying engaged, anticipating needs, and delivering ongoing value.

This chapter focuses on how to transform clients into lifelong partners by using techniques such as personalized follow-ups, proactive problem-solving, and consistent value delivery. By mastering retention as a skill, you'll ensure your clients not only remain loyal but also become advocates for your brand.

Why Retention Matters

Retention isn't just good business—it's essential for growth:

1. **Cost Efficiency:** Retaining an existing client is far less expensive than acquiring a new one.

2. **Increased Lifetime Value (LTV):** Long-term relationships lead to upselling, cross-selling, and ongoing revenue.

3. **Referrals and Advocacy:** Satisfied clients are more likely to recommend your product or service to others.

Example:

A software provider consistently checks in with their clients post-implementation, offering usage tips and insights. This support not only helps clients maximize the tool's value but also creates a foundation for upselling additional features.

Key Strategies for Retention

1. Personalized Follow-Ups

Building meaningful connections requires personalized, thoughtful follow-ups that go beyond generic check-ins.

How to Personalize Follow-Ups:

- **Reference Past Conversations:** Mention specific goals, challenges, or interests the client shared previously.

Example: *"Last time we spoke, you mentioned wanting to reduce downtime by 15%. How's that going so far?"*

- **Acknowledge Milestones:** Celebrate client successes, anniversaries, or other achievements.

Example: *"Congratulations on reaching your first quarter goals! It's been great to see how our solution has supported your progress."*

2. Anticipate Future Needs

Anticipating what your client might need next positions you as a proactive partner rather than a reactive vendor.

How to Anticipate Needs:

- **Monitor Trends:** Stay informed about industry changes that might impact your client's priorities.

Example: *"I noticed new regulations are being discussed in your industry. Let's talk about how we can help you stay compliant."*

- **Engage in Strategic Conversations:** Regularly discuss long-term goals to identify upcoming challenges or opportunities.

Example: *"As you plan for next year, have you considered scaling this solution across your other departments?"*

3. Deliver Ongoing Value

Retention relies on consistently providing value beyond the initial sale. Keep demonstrating why your partnership matters.

How to Deliver Value:

- **Provide Insights:** Share industry reports, case studies, or relevant data to keep clients informed and engaged.

Example: *"I came across this report on emerging trends in your sector and thought you'd find it useful. "*

- **Offer Exclusive Benefits:** Reward loyalty with access to beta features, special events, or personalized training.

Example: *"We're offering early access to our newest feature, and I'd love for you to try it out before the official launch."*

4. Be Proactive About Problem-Solving

Even the strongest relationships encounter challenges. Addressing issues promptly and effectively strengthens trust.

How to Be Proactive:

- **Identify Pain Points Early**: Check in regularly to uncover and resolve issues before they escalate.

Example: *"Are there any areas where the solution isn't meeting your expectations? Let's address them right away."*

- **Follow Through:** Ensure promised fixes or adjustments are completed on time.

Example: *"The update we discussed has been implemented. Let me know if there's anything else we can improve."*

Retention in Action

SCENARIO 1: Personalized Support

A logistics company struggling with user adoption received tailored training sessions from their account manager, who remembered this was a concern from their initial conversations. The personalized approach boosted usage rates and strengthened the relationship.

SCENARIO 2: Anticipating Growth

A marketing agency's account manager noticed a client's social media engagement had increased dramatically. They proactively suggested an analytics tool to help the client optimize their efforts, securing an upsell while demonstrating value.

SCENARIO 3: Resolving Issues with Care

A client expressed frustration with delayed reports. The salesperson not only expedited the fix but also offered a complimentary dashboard training to enhance efficiency, turning a negative experience into a trust-building opportunity.

Workshop
Activities

Activity 1: Crafting Personalized Follow-Ups

1. Provide participants with fictional client scenarios, including recent interactions and goals.

2. Ask participants to draft personalized follow-up emails or messages based on the provided details.

3. Share and discuss which messages felt most authentic and effective.

Activity 2: Anticipating Needs

1. Assign participants a client profile, including industry trends and business goals.

2. Have them brainstorm ways to anticipate and address future needs.

3. Present ideas as a group and refine strategies based on feedback.

Activity 3: Problem-Solving Role-Play

1. Pair participants for a role-play exercise where one acts as a client with a specific issue (e.g., dissatisfaction with a feature).

2. The other participant practices addressing the issue proactively and following through

3. with a solution. Rotate roles and provide constructive feedback on the interaction.

Conclusion

Retention is about more than keeping clients—it's about building lasting partnerships rooted in trust, value, and proactive support. By mastering the art of personalized follow-ups, anticipating future needs, and delivering ongoing value, you'll create relationships that drive long-term success. Like a skilled tactician, you'll position yourself as an indispensable ally, ensuring your clients not only stay but thrive with your support.

CHAPTER 24

Becoming Their Go-To Operative

> *True success lies in becoming indispensable—solve problems proactively and position yourself as a trusted advisor.*

In sales, the ultimate goal isn't just closing deals—it's becoming the person your clients turn to whenever they need advice, solutions, or insight. Like an operative who builds trust to become an indispensable contact, you can position yourself as a trusted advisor by consistently demonstrating unique value and solving problems proactively. By doing so, you'll cement your role as their go-to operative, ensuring long-term loyalty and deepening the relationship with every interaction.

This chapter focuses on how to elevate your role from vendor to indispensable advisor, with actionable strategies, real-world examples, and workshop activities to help you master this transformation.

Why Becoming the Go-To Matters

1. **Client Retention:** Trusted advisors are rarely replaced, even in competitive markets.

2. **Opportunities for Growth:** Clients who trust you will naturally bring you more opportunities for upselling, cross-selling, and referrals.

3. **Stronger Partnerships:** You'll build deeper, more collaborative relationships by positioning yourself as a valued ally.

Example:

A manufacturing client constantly called their account manager for advice on operational efficiency–not just about the product they purchased. This deepened their reliance on the salesperson and led to additional contracts and referrals.

Key Strategies to Become Their Go-To Operative

1. Demonstrate Unique Value

Clients will turn to you if you consistently provide insights or solutions they can't get elsewhere.

How to Demonstrate Value:

- **Offer Industry-Specific Expertise:** Stay informed about trends, challenges, and opportunities in your client's sector.

  Example: *"I noticed a new regulation affecting your industry. Here's how our solution can help you stay compliant."*

- **Share Actionable Insights:** Provide data or ideas they can act on immediately.

  Example: *"Your usage data shows a drop in efficiency on Tuesdays. Let's explore why that might be happening and address it."*

2. Solve Problems Proactively

Proactive problem-solving shows that you're invested in their success, not just the sale.

How to Solve Problems Proactively:

- **Identify Potential Issues Early:** Anticipate challenges before the client does.

  Example: *"I noticed your team hasn't activated this feature yet. Can I walk you throughhow it can save time?"*

- **Provide Tailored Solutions:** Customize your recommendations to address their specificcneeds.

  Example: *"Your business expansion aligns with our*

newest feature. Let's discuss how it can help streamline your new locations."

3. Build Personal Rapport

Clients are more likely to view you as a trusted advisor if you take the time to understand their goals, challenges, and preferences on a personal level.

How to Build Rapport:

- Ask About Their Goals: Show genuine interest in their professional and organizational objectives.

Example: *"What's your biggest priority for the next quarter, and how can I help you achieve it?"*

- **Stay Connected:** Celebrate milestones and acknowledge challenges to maintain an ongoing dialogue.

Example: *"Congratulations on your company's recent award! That's an amazing accomplishment."*

4. Be Consistent and Reliable

Clients will only turn to you if they trust that you'll follow through on your promises.

How to Be Reliable:

- **Communicate Clearly:** Provide timely updates and set realistic expectations.

Example: *"I'll have the revised proposal to you by Thursday afternoon."*

- **Deliver Results:** Ensure your recommendations deliver tangible outcomes.

Example: *"The new integration should reduce your team's workload by 10 hours a week. Let's track its performance over the next month."*

5. Position Yourself as a Strategic Partner

Move beyond transactional interactions by aligning your efforts with their long-term goals.

How to Act as a Strategic Partner:

- **Participate in Planning:** Offer input during their planning sessions or strategic reviews.

Example: *"As you prepare for next year's growth targets, let's explore how this feature can help you scale more efficiently."*

- **Collaborate on Solutions:** Involve yourself in their decision-making processes to demonstrate commitment.

Example: *"Would you like me to join your team's next meeting to answer any technical questions?"*

Becoming the Go-To Operative in Action

SCENARIO 1: Offering Unique Insights

A retail client was struggling with inventory management. Their account manager proactively shared a whitepaper on optimizing inventory processes, along with specific recommendations tailored to their business. The client credited the insights with boosting efficiency and began consulting the salesperson regularly.

SCENARIO 2: Proactively Solving Problems

A client mentioned frustration with low adoption rates for a new tool. Before the client could escalate the issue, their salesperson arranged a training session for the client's team, improving usage rates and cementing the relationship.

SCENARIO 3: Acting as a Strategic Partner

A prospect considering a competitor returned to a trusted salesperson because of their consistent, actionable advice during initial conversations. The salesperson's commitment to their success made them the obvious choice.

Workshop

Activities

Activity 1: Crafting Unique Value Propositions

1. Assign participants a fictional client profile, including their industry and challenges.

2. Participants brainstorm and present tailored insights or recommendations that demonstrate unique value.

3. Discuss which approaches were most effective and why.

Activity 2: Problem-Solving Scenarios

1. Provide participants with a list of common client challenges (e.g., low adoption rates, budget constraints).

2. Participants role-play solving the issue proactively, positioning themselves as trusted advisors.

3. Rotate roles and provide feedback on creativity and effectiveness.

Activity 3: Strategic Partner Role-Play

1. Assign participants the role of a strategic partner in a mock planning session with a client.

2. Participants offer ideas and solutions aligned with the client's goals.

3. Discuss how well their input added value and strengthened the relationship.

Conclusion

Becoming a client's go-to operative is about more than solving immediate problems—it's about demonstrating consistent value, anticipating future needs, and aligning your efforts with their long-term goals. By mastering these skills, you'll position yourself as an indispensable partner, ensuring your clients rely on you for advice, solutions, and support. As their trusted advisor, you'll create relationships that go beyond transactions, driving loyalty, growth, and mutual success.

MASTERING THE SALES MINDSET

Success in sales begins with the right mindset. Section 7, **Mastering the Sales Mindset**, explores the psychological principles and mental frameworks that drive top-tier performance. Borrowing from the resilience and discipline of Intelligence officers, this section helps you build the mental toughness, strategic thinking, and adaptive skills needed to thrive in a competitive environment. In this section, you'll learn how to overcome challenges, embrace growth, and cultivate leadership qualities that set you apart in your field. By mastering the sales mindset, you'll not only achieve your goals but also inspire and empower those around you.

CHAPTER 25

Operative-Level Resilience

> **"**
>
> *Rejection isn't the end—it's the beginning of growth. Resilience turns setbacks into stepping stones for success.*
>
> **"**

Sales is a profession that demands resilience. Just like an operative navigating high-stakes missions, sales professionals must remain composed under pressure, adapt to setbacks, and recover quickly from rejection. Building mental toughness is not only essential for sustaining long-term success but also for maintaining a positive mindset in the face of challenges.

This chapter explores strategies for cultivating operative-level resilience, helping you handle stress, bounce back from rejection, and stay focused on your goals. Through actionable techniques and examples, you'll learn how to thrive under pressure and turn setbacks into opportunities for growth.

Why Resilience is Critical in Sales

1. **Rejection is Inevitable:** Even the most skilled salespeople face objections and lost deals. Resilience helps you move forward without losing confidence.

2. **High-Pressure Environments:** Deadlines, quotas, and competitive markets create stress. Resilience enables you to stay calm and perform at your best.

3. **Adaptation is Key:** The ability to pivot and adjust your strategy is essential when plans don't go as expected.

Example:
A salesperson loses a major deal after months of effort. Instead of dwelling on the loss, they review the process, identify areas for improvement, and apply those lessons to their next opportunity, which they successfully close.

Building Operative-Level Resilience

1. Reframe Rejection

Rejection isn't personal—it's a natural part of the sales process. Viewing it as an opportunity to learn and grow can shift your perspective.

How to Reframe Rejection:

- **Focus on Feedback:** Use rejection as a chance to understand what didn't work.

  Example: *"I appreciate your honesty. Could you share what factors influenced your decision?"*

- **Celebrate Effort Over Outcome:** Recognize the progress you've made, even if the deal didn't close.

  Example: *"I didn't win this one, but I successfully built rapport with a key decision-maker."*

2. Develop Emotional Intelligence

Understanding and managing your emotions is key to maintaining composure under pressure. Emotional intelligence also helps you empathize with prospects and colleagues, building stronger relationships.

Strategies for Emotional Intelligence:

- **Self-Awareness:** Recognize your stress triggers and how they affect your behavior.

  Example: Notice if a high-pressure deadline makes you overly aggressive in follow-ups, and adjust accordingly.

- **Empathy:** Put yourself in the prospect's shoes to better understand their concerns.

  Example: *"I sense that the timing feels overwhelming. Let's revisit this when things settle down."*

3. Build a Resilience Routine

Daily habits and routines can help you maintain mental toughness and bounce back from setbacks more quickly.

Elements of a Resilience Routine:

- Physical Health: Regular exercise, sleep, and nutrition boost your energy and stress tolerance.

Example: A quick walk before a high-stakes meeting can calm nerves and sharpen focus.

- Mental Breaks: Schedule time for mindfulness or relaxation to recharge.

Example: Spend five minutes meditating between calls to reset your mindset.

- **Reflect and Reset:** Dedicate time at the end of each day to review what went well and what can improve.

Example: *"I handled the objection on pricing well today. Tomorrow, I'll refine my pitch on ROI."*

4. Cultivate a Growth Mindset

A growth mindset sees challenges as opportunities to improve rather than insurmountable obstacles. Embracing this perspective helps you stay motivated and resilient.

How to Foster a Growth Mindset:

- **Embrace Challenges:** View difficult prospects or situations as opportunities to sharpen your skills.

> **Example:** "This client is demanding, but if I can meet their expectations, I can handle anyone."

- **Celebrate Progress:** Recognize small wins to maintain momentum and build confidence.

> **Example:** "I didn't close the deal today, but I moved it further along the pipeline."

5. Build a Support Network

Having a network of mentors, peers, and colleagues to share experiences and advice can bolster your resilience.

How to Leverage Your Network:

- **Seek Feedback:** Ask trusted colleagues for constructive criticism.

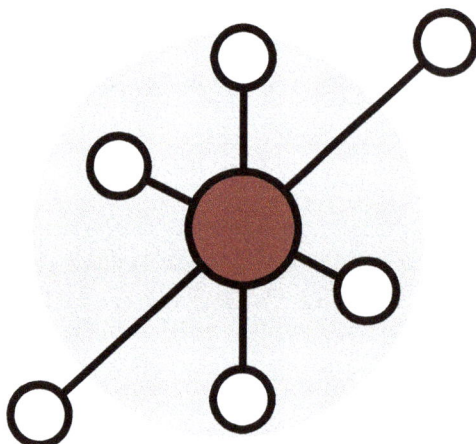

> **Example:** "How did I handle that objection in the meeting? What could I have done differently?"

- **Share Challenges:** Discussing setbacks with peers can provide new perspectives and solutions.

> **Example:** "Have you encountered a client with similar objections? How did you handle it?"

Resilience in Action

SCENARIO 1: Handling Stress During Negotiations

A prospect challenges every detail of a proposal. Instead of reacting emotionally, the salesperson takes a deep breath, listens attentively, and reframes the conversation around shared goals. The calm approach leads to a productive discussion and a signed contract.

SCENARIO 2: Bouncing Back from Rejection

After losing a deal to a competitor, a salesperson follows up with the prospect to ask for feedback. They learn the competitor offered a feature their company lacks. Armed with this insight, they adjust their future pitches to highlight their unique strengths, securing a similar client soon after.

SCENARIO 3: Thriving Under Quota Pressure

Facing an end-of-quarter sales goal, a salesperson schedules focused work blocks, prioritizes high-probability leads, and practices mindfulness between calls to stay composed. They meet their target without burning out.

Workshop
Activities

Activity 1: Rejection Reframing

1. Provide participants with common rejection scenarios (e.g., *"Your price is too high"*).

2. Have them write a response that focuses on extracting feedback and maintaining a positive outlook.

3. Discuss how the reframing changes the perception of rejection and fosters growth.

Activity 2: Emotional Intelligence Role-Play

1. Pair participants and assign one as a stressed-out prospect and the other as the salesperson.

2. The salesperson practices recognizing emotional cues and responding empathetically.

3. Rotate roles and provide feedback on the effectiveness of the responses.

Activity 3: Building a Resilience Plan

1. Ask participants to outline a daily or weekly routine that incorporates physical health, mental breaks, and reflection.

2. Share routines in small groups and discuss how these practices can strengthen resilience.

Conclusion

Resilience is the backbone of long-term success in sales. By reframing rejection, cultivating emotional intelligence, and developing consistent routines, you can stay composed, adaptable, and focused under pressure. With a growth mindset and strong support network, every setback becomes a stepping stone toward improvement. Like a skilled operative, your ability to maintain mental toughness will set you apart and ensure sustained success in even the most challenging environments.

CHAPTER 26

Continuous Improvement

"

Excellence is built through reflection and refinement—commit to learning, adapting, and evolving every day.

"

In sales, the best professionals never stop learning. Success comes from refining your skills, embracing feedback, and constantly adapting to new challenges. Just like an operative analyzes every mission to improve future outcomes, sales professionals must adopt feedback loops, practice self-reflection, and nurture a growth mindset to stay ahead.

This chapter provides strategies to embed continuous improvement into your routine, helping you identify areas for growth, act on constructive feedback, and consistently elevate your performance. By adopting a mindset of lifelong learning, you'll ensure sustained success in an ever-changing sales environment.

Why Continuous Improvement Matters

1. **Keeps You Competitive:** The sales landscape evolves rapidly, and continuous learning ensures you stay ahead of industry trends and competitor tactics.

2. **Builds Resilience:** Regular self-assessment helps you adapt to setbacks and turn challenges into opportunities for growth.

3. **Enhances Client Relationships:** By improving your skills, you'll better understand and meet client needs, strengthening trust and loyalty.

Example:

A salesperson struggling with handling objections attends a workshop on negotiation skills. After applying the techniques, they successfully close deals with clients who previously seemed hesitant.

Key Strategies for Continuous Improvement

1. Embrace Feedback Loops

Feedback is one of the most powerful tools for improvement. Actively seek input from clients, colleagues, and managers to identify blind spots and refine your approach.

How to Create Feedback Loops:

- **From Clients:** After a sale, ask what they valued most and where you could improve.

  Example: *"What did you find most helpful during our conversations, and is there anything I could have done differently?"*

- **From Peers and Managers:** Request feedback on your performance during team meetings or one-on-one reviews.

  Example: *"Do you think I handled that objection effectively? How could I improve my response?"*

2. Practice Self-Reflection

Regularly evaluating your performance helps you identify patterns, strengths, and areas for growth.

How to Reflect Effectively:

- **Post-Call Reviews:** After each sales interaction, ask yourself:
  » What went well?
  » What could I have done differently?
  » What can I apply to my next conversation?

- **End-of-Week Reviews:** Summarize key successes and challenges from the week to track progress over time.

  Example:
  A salesperson notices during self-reflection that they often rush to close deals, missing opportunities to build rapport. They adjust their approach in future calls, leading to stronger client relationships.

3. Cultivate a Growth Mindset

A growth mindset emphasizes learning and adaptability, viewing challenges as opportunities to improve rather than obstacles to avoid.

How to Develop a Growth Mindset:

- **Learn from Failures:** Instead of dwelling on lost deals, focus on what you can take away.

    Example: *"The client chose a competitor because of their pricing. Next time, I'll emphasize ROI more clearly to show value."*

- **Set Development Goals:** Create specific, measurable goals for skills you want to improve.

    Example: *"I will practice handling objections by role-playing twice a week with a colleague."*

4. Invest in Professional Development

Continuous improvement requires actively seeking opportunities to learn new skills and deepen your expertise.

How to Invest in Growth:

- **Attend Training Sessions:** Join workshops, webinars, or industry events to expand your knowledge.

- **Read and Research:** Stay informed by reading books, articles, and case studies related to sales and your industry.

- **Practice New Skills:** Apply what you learn immediately to reinforce your understanding.

Example:

A salesperson attends a seminar on storytelling in sales and starts incorporating narratives into their pitches. As a result, they notice increased engagement from prospects.

5. Measure and Celebrate Progress

Tracking your growth over time motivates you to stay committed and highlights how far you've come.

How to Measure Progress:

- **Track Metrics:** Monitor key performance indicators (KPIs) such as conversion rates, average deal size, and client retention.

- **Celebrate Milestones:** Acknowledge when you hit goals or make noticeable improvements.

Example:

After setting a goal to improve follow-up consistency, a salesperson tracks their progress and sees a 20% increase in closed deals within three months.

Continuous Improvement in Action

SCENARIO 1: Turning Feedback into Action

A prospect mentions that a salesperson's demo felt too technical. Instead of being defensive, the salesperson thanks them for the feedback and practices simplifying their pitch. In the next demo, they receive positive feedback for being clear and concise.

SCENARIO 2: Learning from a Lost Deal

After losing a deal, a salesperson reflects on the experience and realizes they didn't address the client's budget concerns early enough. They adjust their discovery process to include budget discussions upfront, improving their close rate.

SCENARIO 3: Celebrating Small Wins

A salesperson sets a goal to improve their email response time to under 24 hours. After successfully meeting this goal for a month, they reward themselves and share their success with their team, reinforcing the habit.

Workshop
Activities

Activity 1: Feedback Action Plans

1. Pair participants and have them share a recent sales experience where they faced challenges.

2. The partner provides constructive feedback and suggestions for improvement.

3. Participants create an action plan to implement the feedback and share it with the group.

Activity 2: Self-Reflection Journaling

1. Ask participants to write down answers to the

following questions after a mock sales call:

- What went well?
- What didn't go as planned?
- What will I do differently next time?

2. Discuss reflections in small groups and identify common themes for growth.

Activity 3: Growth Mindset Role-Play

1. Present participants with challenging scenarios (e.g., a prospect choosing a competitor).

2. Participants practice reframing the challenge as a learning opportunity and outlining steps to improve.

3. Share insights and strategies as a group.

Conclusion

Continuous improvement is the cornerstone of long-term success in sales. By embracing feedback, practicing self-reflection, and fostering a growth mindset, you'll refine your skills and adapt to new challenges with confidence. With each lesson learned and skill mastered, you'll not only improve your performance but also strengthen your reputation as a trusted, capable professional. The journey of growth never ends, and by committing to it, you'll ensure your success in an ever-changing sales environment.

CHAPTER 27

Thinking Like an Operative, Acting Like a Sales Leader

> *Sales leaders think strategically and lead by example—empower others while continuously elevating your craft.*

Sales leadership is not just about hitting targets; it's about leading by example, inspiring others, and building a legacy of success. By integrating intelligence officer inspired strategies into your daily practice, you can elevate yourself as both a top performer and a mentor to others. This chapter explores how to apply the principles of tactical thinking, strategic planning, and people-focused leadership to rise as a true sales leader in your field.

Why Operative Thinking is Crucial for Leadership

Intelligence officers excel by combining tactical precision with strategic foresight. Applying this mindset in sales leadership helps you:

1. **Master Complex Scenarios:** Navigate challenges with clarity and confidence.

2. **Inspire Teams:** Model resilience, adaptability, and problem-solving for others.

3. **Achieve Long-Term Success:** Think beyond individual wins to build sustainable growth and team success.

Example:

A sales leader identifies a competitor's aggressive tactics in a new market. By analyzing the competitor's moves, anticipating client concerns, and coaching their team to emphasize unique value propositions, they capture market share while fostering team growth.

How to Think Like an Operative and Lead Like a Sales Professional

1. Integrate Strategic Thinking into Daily Practices

Effective leaders view every task as part of a bigger picture. Analyze your activities and align them with long-term goals.

How to Apply Strategic Thinking:

- Anticipate Market Changes: Stay ahead by monitoring industry trends and evolving client needs.

Example: *"With new sustainability regulations emerging, let's pivot our pitch to highlight our eco-friendly solutions."*

- Plan Beyond the Quarter: Set long-term goals that guide your short-term actions.

Example: *"Our goal is to become the leading provider in this sector within two years. This quarter, we'll focus on building key partnerships."*

2. Lead with Tactical Precision

As a leader, your ability to execute plans with precision sets the tone for your team. Operative thinking helps you approach challenges methodically.

Tactical Leadership in Action:

- **Break Down Challenges:** Simplify complex problems into actionable steps.

Example: *"We're behind on our quarterly goal. Let's focus on upselling existing clients in the next two weeks."*

- **Adapt Mid-Mission:** Be ready to adjust when circumstances change.

Example: If a major client delays a decision, redirect resources to high-probability leads to make up for lost momentum.

3. Build a High-Performing Team

True leaders empower others to succeed. Share your expertise, foster collaboration, and create a culture of excellence.

How to Empower Your Team:

- **Mentor Actively:** Share insights from your successes and failures to guide others.

  Example: *"When I handled a similar objection, I found that focusing on ROI rather than features made all the difference."*

- **Celebrate Wins:** Recognize individual and team achievements to build morale.

  Example: *"This deal closed because of Sarah's persistence and strategic thinking—great job!"*

4. Focus on Relationship-Building

Just as operatives rely on networks of trusted allies, sales leaders build strong relationships with clients, team members, and industry peers.

How to Build Relationships:

- **Strengthen Client Trust:** Act as a strategic partner to clients, ensuring long-term loyalty.

  Example: *"We've worked together for three years now— let's discuss how we can continue to grow together in the next phase."*

- **Foster Collaboration:** Encourage teamwork within your sales organization.

> **Example:** *"Let's brainstorm as a team on how we can refine our approach to these challenging prospects."*

5. Model Resilience and Growth

Leaders face rejection and setbacks alongside their teams. Demonstrating resilience inspires confidence and encourages continuous improvement.

How to Model Resilience:

- **Stay Composed Under Pressure:** Respond calmly to challenges, setting an example for others.

> **Example:** *"This quarter was tough, but let's focus on what we've learned and how we can improve."*

- **Encourage a Growth Mindset:** Promote learning and adaptation as part of your team's culture.

> **Example:** *"Let's analyze why this deal didn't close and brainstorm new approaches for similar prospects."*

Becoming a Leader in Action

SCENARIO 1: Turning Challenges into Opportunities

A competitor undercuts pricing in a key market. Instead of reacting defensively, the sales leader guides their team to focus on long-term value and customer success stories, winning client trust and new deals.

SCENARIO 2: Mentoring Through Objections

A junior salesperson struggles with handling objections. The leader shares specific techniques, role-plays scenarios, and provides actionable feedback. Within weeks, the salesperson gains confidence and closes their first major deal.

SCENARIO 3: Building a Collaborative Culture

A team faces a challenging sales target. The leader organizes a workshop where everyone shares strategies, successes, and lessons learned. This collaborative effort boosts morale and drives new ideas that lead to surpassing the target.

Workshop
Activities

Activity 1: Strategic Problem-Solving

1. 1. 2. 3. Divide participants into small groups and present them with a complex sales challenge (e.g., a competitor's aggressive pricing strategy).
2. Groups develop a strategic plan to address the challenge, focusing on long-term goals.
3. Each group presents their plan, and the facilitator provides feedback on strategic thinking.

Activity 2: Tactical Coaching Role-Play

1. Pair participants as a leader and a team member.
2. The "team member" presents a challenge (e.g., struggling to close a deal).

3. The "leader" provides coaching and actionable advice using tactical precision.

4. Rotate roles and discuss the effectiveness of each coaching session.

Activity 3: Resilience and Growth Planning

1. Ask participants to reflect on a recent setback and write down:

   » What went wrong.

   » What they learned.

   » How they will apply those lessons moving forward.

2. Share insights in small groups to promote a culture of resilience and growth.

Conclusion

To think like an operative and act like a sales leader is to combine tactical precision with strategic foresight while empowering others to succeed. By integrating intelligence officer inspired principles into your daily practice, you'll not only achieve your own goals but also inspire those around you to thrive. As a mentor, strategist, and resilient role model, you'll leave a lasting impact—both on your clients and your team—cementing your legacy as a true leader in your field.

HARNESSING PSYCHOLOGICAL INSIGHT

Congratulate yourself for making it this far and get ready for the art and science of strategic interaction in sales. This last section is a **bonus section** and offers a toolkit for understanding and influencing people. Here, you will walk through a series of methodologies adapted from espionage and psychology, but tailored to empower sales professionals to excel in their craft. These are topics to read through a few times, but before you know it, you will master the nuances of human behavior and strategic foresight and know the right framework to apply to any given situation.

CHAPTER 28

The Framework of Influence – Spycraft Models for Sales Success

> "
>
> *Mastering influence in sales requires the precision of spycraft: understanding motivations, prioritizing targets, and executing strategies with the clarity and determination of a seasoned agent.*
>
> "

In this chapter, we explore a series of powerful frameworks drawn from espionage and behavioral science, tailored to enhance your capabilities in sales through strategic influence and persuasion. Each model is introduced through a compelling scenario, broken down into its strategic components, applied to sales, and accompanied by actionable steps.

MICE Framework
(Motivations for Doing Anything)

Every decision a person makes, whether consciously or subconsciously, is driven by motivation. In sales, understanding these motivators is key to creating pitches that resonate, building trust, and ultimately closing deals. The MICE Framework—an acronym for Money, Ideology, Coercion, and Ego—was originally developed as a tool in espionage to understand and influence individuals. Applied to sales, it becomes a powerful lens through which to decode the "why" behind every prospect's behavior, allowing you to craft personalized approaches that align with their deepest motivations.

This chapter explores how each element of the MICE Framework can be used to uncover and address what matters most to your clients. By analyzing their motivators and tailoring your approach accordingly, you can gain a competitive edge in any sales conversation.

The Four Pillars of Motivation in the MICE Framework

1. Money (Financial Gain or Savings)

The first and often most obvious motivator is money. Clients driven by this motivator are focused on tangible financial benefits, such as cost savings, increased revenue, or a strong return on investment (ROI).

How to Identify:

- They ask questions about pricing, cost-effectiveness, or ROI.
- Their organization emphasizes budget constraints or financial metrics in discussions.

Sales Approach:

- Highlight features that save money or increase efficiency.
- Provide data on ROI, cost reductions, or long-term savings.
- Use case studies or testimonials that showcase financial outcomes.

Example:

A software vendor pitching an enterprise solution emphasizes how their platform will reduce operational costs by 30% within the first year. They back this claim with data from a similar-sized client who achieved significant savings.

2. Ideology (Beliefs, Values, and Ethics)

Clients motivated by ideology care deeply about aligning their decisions with their personal or organizational values. These may include social responsibility, environmental sustainability, or ethical practices.

How to Identify:

- They reference their company's mission or core values in conversations.
- They express strong opinions about ethical or societal issues.

Sales Approach:

- Align your product or service with their stated values.
- Emphasize any sustainable, ethical, or socially responsible aspects of your offering.
- Be prepared to demonstrate how your solution contributes to the greater good.

Example:

A pharmaceutical sales representative pitching a new drug to a clinic emphasizes how the drug improves patient outcomes and aligns with the clinic's mission of prioritizing patient welfare over profit.

3. Coercion (Avoiding Risk or Pressure)

Coercion isn't about manipulation but rather understanding the pressures and risks influencing your client. Clients motivated by coercion seek to avoid potential negative outcomes, whether professional, financial, or reputational.

How to Identify:

- They express concerns about potential risks, compliance, or competitive threats.
- Their tone or questions indicate hesitation or anxiety about making the wrong decision.

Sales Approach:

- Position your product as a solution to minimize risks or pressures.
- Address concerns directly and provide assurances, such as warranties or guarantees.

- Offer insights about how your solution protects them from competitors or external risks.

4. Ego (Recognition, Status, and Self-Perception)

Ego-driven clients seek validation, recognition, or status. They want solutions that make them look good to peers, superiors, or the industry at large.

How to Identify:

- They talk about their personal achievements or their company's reputation.
- They are drawn to prestige, exclusivity, or high-end features.

Sales Approach:

- Frame your product or service as a way for them to stand out or achieve recognition.
- Highlight exclusivity, premium features, or industry-leading benefits.
- Personalize your approach to make them feel valued and important.

make it a symbol of success, appealing directly to the prospect's desire for status.

Applying the MICE Framework in Sales

To make the most of the MICE Framework, follow these three steps:

1. Identify Key Decision-Makers

Understand the hierarchy and structure of the client organization. Identify not only who makes the final decision but also who influences the decision-making process.

2. Hypothesize Motivators

Using research, observation, and conversations, assess which MICE motivators are most likely driving each decision-maker. Keep in mind that different individuals within the same organization may have varying priorities.

3. Personalize Your Pitch

Tailor your messaging to address the motivators you've identified. For example:

- **For Money**, highlight cost savings and ROI.
- **For Ideology**, focus on ethical or mission-aligned aspects.
- **For Coercion**, emphasize risk mitigation and compliance.
- **For Ego**, showcase exclusivity and prestige.

The Pharmaceutical Sales Rep

A pharmaceutical sales representative is promoting a new drug to a clinic. Through observation and research, they discover that the head physician is motivated by patient outcomes *(Ideology)* while the clinic's administrator is focused on cost savings *(Money)*.

Action Plan:

- For the physician, they highlight how the drug improves long-term patient health and aligns with the clinic's mission of prioritizing care.

- For the administrator, they present data showing how the drug reduces hospital readmissions, resulting in significant cost savings.

By addressing both motivators, the rep secures buy-in from both stakeholders and closes the deal.

Workshop
Activities

Activity 1: Motivator Mapping

- Divide participants into groups. Each group receives a hypothetical client scenario with a detailed profile.

- Groups identify the key decision-makers and hypothesize their primary MICE motivators.

- Each group presents their analysis and suggests tailored approaches based on the identified motivators.

Activity 2: Pitch Personalization Challenge

- Participants select a product or service they currently sell.
- Using the MICE Framework, they create four tailored pitches–each targeting one of the MICE motivators.
- Share the pitches with the group and discuss which approach would work best in different scenarios.

Activity 3: Role-Playing Scenarios

- In pairs, one participant acts as the salesperson while the other plays the role of a prospect.
- The prospect is secretly assigned one of the MICE motivators, and the salesperson must identify the motivator through questioning and observation.
- Rotate roles and provide feedback on how well the motivators were identified and addressed.

RASCLS Framework
(Influence and Persuasion)

Sales is, at its heart, the art of persuasion. To win deals, sales professionals must connect with their audience on a psychological level, crafting messages that resonate with human instincts and emotions. The RASCLS Framework—an acronym for Reciprocity, Authority, Scarcity, Commitment, Liking, and Social Proof—is a powerful tool that leverages key psychological principles to influence decisions effectively. By integrating these principles into your sales strategy, you can create compelling pitches that align with your prospects' desires and decision-making patterns.

In this chapter, we'll explore how each element of the RASCLS Framework works, provide actionable strategies for applying them in sales, and present real-world scenarios where these principles have led to success.

Breaking Down the
RASCLS Framework

1. Reciprocity – The Give-and-Take Principle

Reciprocity is one of the most fundamental principles of persuasion. When someone receives something of value, they feel compelled to give something in return. In sales, providing value upfront—whether through free trials, consultations, or useful content—can create a sense of obligation that leads to a purchase.

Scenario Example:

A SaaS company offers a free trial of its premium software. During the trial, they provide hands-on support and resources to ensure the prospect experiences the value firsthand. When the trial ends, the prospect feels a natural inclination to reciprocate by purchasing the software.

How to Use It in Sales:

- Offer free resources, consultations, or trials.
- Personalize your approach to make the prospect feel valued.
- Emphasize how the value you've provided aligns with their needs.

2. Authority – Establishing Expertise

People are naturally inclined to trust and follow those who project authority. By demonstrating expertise and credibility, you position yourself and your solution as reliable and worthy of trust.

Scenario Example:

A cybersecurity company emphasizes its certifications, high-profile clients, and media recognition during a pitch. By highlighting its authority in the field, the company builds trust and overcomes hesitations.

How to Use It in Sales:

- Highlight certifications, credentials, or awards.
- Use case studies and data to back up your claims.
- Position yourself as a trusted advisor, not just a salesperson.

3. Scarcity – The Fear of Missing Out

Scarcity creates urgency by emphasizing limited availability or time-sensitive opportunities. When prospects feel they might lose out, they're more likely to take action.

Scenario Example:

A tech startup emphasizes that only a handful of spots remain in their funding round. By creating urgency, they compel venture capitalists to act quickly, securing investment commitments.

How to Use It in Sales:

- Set deadlines for special offers or discounts.
- Highlight limited inventory or exclusive access.
- Frame your product as a unique opportunity they won't find elsewhere.

4. Commitment – Encouraging Small Agreements

The principle of commitment involves securing small, initial agreements that pave the way for larger commitments. When people take even minor actions, they're more likely to stay consistent with those actions over time.

Scenario Example:

A fitness equipment company asks prospects to sign up for a free webinar about improving home workouts. Those who attend are later more likely to purchase equipment, having already taken an initial step toward engagement.

How to Use It in Sales:

- Start with small asks, such as signing up for a newsletter or attending a demo.
- Use follow-ups to build on previous agreements.

- Reinforce their decisions by aligning the next step with their goals.

5. Liking – Building Personal Connections

People are more likely to say yes to those they like and trust. Liking is cultivated through rapport, shared interests, and genuine empathy.

Scenario Example:

A real estate agent takes time to learn about a family's hobbies and preferences, weaving those into conversations about potential homes. By building a personal connection, the agent becomes the family's trusted advisor.

How to Use It in Sales:

- Find common ground and shared interests with prospects.
- Show genuine empathy for their challenges and goals.
- Be approachable, warm, and authentic in your interactions.

6. Social Proof – The Power of Influence

People are heavily influenced by what others are doing or endorsing. Social proof provides reassurance that they're making the right choice by following the crowd.

Scenario Example:

A software company includes testimonials from high-profile clients on its website and highlights that 90% of Fortune 500 companies use its product. This reassures prospects that the product is a proven solution.

How to Use It in Sales:

- Share testimonials, case studies, and client success stories.

- Highlight metrics, such as the number of users or positive reviews.
- Use endorsements from respected industry figures or organizations.

Applying the RASCLS Framework in Sales

STEP 1: Plan Your Engagement Strategy

Before meeting with a prospect, identify which RASCLS principles are most relevant to their needs and decision-making style. For example:

- A highly analytical buyer may respond well to Authority and Social Proof.
- A status-driven buyer may be more influenced by Scarcity and Liking.

STEP 2: Incorporate Multiple Principles

Combine two or more principles for maximum impact. For instance:

- Use Reciprocity by offering a free trial, followed by Commitment to secure a follow-up meeting.
- Highlight Social Proof with testimonials and create urgency with Scarcity to drive action.

STEP 3: Evaluate and Adjust

After each interaction, assess which principles were most effective and refine your approach for future pitches.

Scenario in Action:
The Tech Startup Pitch

A tech startup is seeking funding from venture capitalists. T o create a persuasive pitch, they incorporate multiple RASCLS principles:

- **Social Proof:** They showcase endorsements from well-known angel investors.

- **Scarcity:** They emphasize that only two spots remain in the funding round.

- **Authority:** They highlight the founders' track record of building successful startups.

The combination of these principles builds trust, creates urgency, and ultimately secures commitments from investors.

Workshop
Activities

Activity 1: RASCLS Role-Play

- **Objective:** Practice applying the RASCLS Framework in a sales scenario.

- **Instructions:**

  1. Divide participants into pairs. One plays the salesperson, and the other acts as the prospect.

2. The salesperson must incorporate at least three RASCLS principles in their pitch.

3. Rotate roles and provide feedback on the effectiveness of the approach.

Activity 2: Framework Mapping

- **Objective:** Identify opportunities to use RASCLS principles in your current sales process.

- **Instructions:**

  1. List your top three prospects or sales opportunities.

  2. Identify which RASCLS principles could be applied to each opportunity.

  3. Share your strategy with the group for input and refinement.

Activity 3: Case Study Breakdown

- **Objective:** Learn how RASCLS principles are applied in real-world sales scenarios.

- **Instructions:**

  1. Provide a detailed case study (real or hypothetical) that showcases the use of RASCLS principles.

  2. In small groups, participants identify which principles were used and how they contributed to the outcome.

  3. Groups present their findings and discuss additional ways to strengthen the strategy.

CARVER Matrix
(Target Selection and Prioritization)

In the world of sales, time is a finite resource. Success depends on focusing your efforts where they will yield the best results. The CARVER Matrix, originally designed by the U.S. military for target evaluation and mission planning, offers a strategic framework for prioritizing sales targets with precision and clarity. By scoring potential leads on key factors, you can systematically identify the most valuable prospects and allocate your resources accordingly.

This chapter will explore how the CARVER Matrix works, how it can be adapted to sales, and how applying it can elevate your targeting strategy, helping you close deals faster and more efficiently.

Breaking Down
the CARVER Matrix

The CARVER Matrix evaluates six key criteria: Criticality, Accessibility, Recuperability, Vulnerability, Effect, and Recognizability. Each criterion helps determine the overall value of a target and the likelihood of achieving success when pursuing that target.

1. Criticality (How Important Is the Target?)

Definition: Criticality measures how essential the target is to your overall sales goals. In sales, this means assessing how much revenue or strategic value a particular lead could bring if closed successfully.

Sales Questions:

- Does closing this deal significantly impact my sales quota?
- Is this target linked to a high-value, long-term account?

Example: A B2B SaaS company considers a major retail chain that could adopt its platform across hundreds of locations. This lead is highly critical because of its large revenue potential.

2. Accessibility (How Easy Is It to Reach the Target?)

Definition: Accessibility measures how easy or difficult it is to engage with the target. In sales, this could mean the availability of decision-makers, responsiveness to outreach, or the simplicity of the buying process.

Sales Questions:

- Are the decision-makers approachable?
- Can I reach them through warm introductions or referrals?

Example: A real estate agent focuses on a corporate client whose decision-making team is highly responsive and schedules meetings quickly—an indicator of high accessibility.

3. Recuperability (How Quickly Can You Recover Costs?)

Definition: Recuperability evaluates how soon you'll recover the investment of time, money, and effort spent on pursuing the target. In sales, this translates to the speed of closing the deal and realizing revenue.

Sales Questions:

- How long is the typical sales cycle for this target?
- When will revenue start flowing if the deal closes?

Example: A consulting firm targets mid-size companies with immediate project needs, knowing these clients will sign contracts quickly and generate fast revenue.

4. Vulnerability (How Susceptible Is the Target?)

Definition: Vulnerability refers to how open or susceptible the target is to your offer. In sales, this means how likely a lead is to switch providers or adopt your solution.

Sales Questions:

- Is the target experiencing pain points or challenges I can solve?
- Are they dissatisfied with current vendors or products?

Example: A managed IT services provider targets businesses struggling with outdated tech infrastructure, making them highly vulnerable to a modern solution.

5. Effect (What Is the Potential Impact of Success?)

Definition: Effect measures the broader impact of securing the target. In sales, this includes the potential for long-term business, future referrals, or industry influence gained by closing the deal.

Sales Questions:

- Will landing this client open doors to other major accounts?
- Could success with this lead boost my company's industry credibility?

Example: A marketing agency targets a well-known global brand, knowing that a successful campaign with them would enhance its portfolio and attract other high-profile clients.

6. Recognizability (How Easy Is It to Identify the Target?)

Definition: Recognizability measures how well you can profile and evaluate the target before engaging. In sales, this refers to how easily you can gather information on the lead's needs, challenges, and buying history.

Sales Questions:

- Is information about the target readily available through public sources, industry reports, or personal networks?
- Can I clearly define their pain points and potential fit for my offering?

Example: A SaaS company targets firms whose business models are well-documented in industry reports, making them easy to profile and approach with tailored pitches.

Applying the CARVER Matrix in Sales

STEP 1: List Potential Targets

Begin by listing all current leads, prospects, or potential clients. Include any active deals or high-value prospects still in the pipeline.

STEP 2: Score Each Target on the CARVER Scale

Use a scale of 1 to 5 (or 1 to 10) to rate each target on the six CARVER criteria. Assign scores based on objective data, market research, and historical performance.

Scoring Example:

TARGET	Cr	Ac	Rc	Vl	Ef	Rn	Total Score
Retail Chain A	5	4	3	5	5	4	26
Mid-Market Tech Firm B	3	3	4	4	4	5	23

Cr: credibility, Ac: Accessibility. Rc: Recuperability, Vl: Vulnerability, Ef: Effect, Rn: Recognizability

Step 3: Prioritize High-Scoring Targets

Focus your sales efforts on the targets with the highest total scores. These leads have the greatest potential for success with the least amount of effort and risk.

Step 4: Allocate Resources

Assign your top-performing sales team members to the most promising leads, ensuring that high-scoring targets receive maximum attention.

A real estate agency uses the CARVER Matrix to determine which commercial property listings to focus on during a busy sales quarter.

- **Criticality:** A large shopping center represents the biggest potential commission.

- **Accessibility:** The property's owner is easily reachable and has expressed interest in selling.

- **Recuperability:** The firm expects a fast closing timeline.

- **Vulnerability:** The owner is struggling to lease vacant spaces, making them motivated to sell.

- **Effect:** Successfully selling the property would boost the agency's reputation in the commercial real estate sector.

- **Recognizability:** Public records provide detailed information on the property's valuation and ownership structure. After scoring multiple properties, the agency assigns its senior sales agents to this listing, focusing resources where success is most likely.

Workshop

Activities

Activity 1: Target Scoring Challenge
- **Objective:** Apply the CARVER Matrix to real-world sales scenarios.

- **Instructions:**
  1. Divide into teams and receive a list of five potential sales targets.
  2. Score each target using the CARVER criteria.
  3. Present findings, justifying the scores and suggesting next steps.

Activity 2: Live Lead Evaluation

- **Objective:** Evaluate actual leads from your sales pipeline.
- **Instructions:**
  1. Sales reps select active leads from their pipeline.
  2. Evaluate each lead using the CARVER criteria.
  3. Discuss next steps based on each lead's total score.

Activity 3: CARVER Planning Workshop

- **Objective:** Build a strategic sales action plan.
- **Instructions:**
  1. Develop a detailed action plan for the highest-ranked target.
  2. Assign specific tasks based on identified strengths and vulnerabilities.
  3. Present the strategy to the larger group for feedback.

SADR Model
(Target Exploitation and Engagement)

In sales, identifying and securing high-value clients requires more than just good instincts—it demands a structured, strategic approach. The **SADR** Model—an acronym for **Spot, Assess, Develop, and Recruit**—originates from the world of intelligence operations, where its purpose is to identify and engage valuable human assets. In sales, this model offers a systematic process for finding, evaluating, nurturing, and ultimately converting top-tier prospects into long-term clients.

This chapter will explore each phase of the SADR Model, breaking down how you can apply its principles to maximize your sales success. We'll illustrate how SADR works through real-world sales scenarios, provide actionable strategies, and include workshop activities to reinforce the learning process.

The Four Stages
of the SADR Model

1. Spot – Identify Potential Prospects

The first stage of the SADR Model is Spotting—finding potential leads who fit your ideal customer profile (ICP). This step involves conducting research, leveraging market intelligence, and identifying companies or individuals with high potential for long-term business relationships.

Key Tactics:

- Conduct industry research and trend analysis.
- Use LinkedIn, company databases, and CRM tools to find prospects.
- Attend industry events and trade shows.
- Monitor competitor activity to identify potential leads.

Sales Scenario Example:

A business consultant specializing in supply chain optimization monitors industry reports and notices that a mid-size retail chain is expanding its logistics operations. Recognizing a potential need for improved supply chain management, they add the company to their list of leads.

Action Plan:

1. Create a lead list based on industry or market-specific criteria.
2. Prioritize leads with growth indicators, such as recent funding rounds or market expansions.
3. Use sales intelligence tools to track emerging opportunities.

2. Assess – Evaluate Prospect Potential

Once you've identified leads, the next step is Assessing their potential. This involves qualifying leads by evaluating how well they fit your offering, their buying capacity, decision-making process, and the challenges they face.

Assessment Criteria:

- **Budget:** Can they afford your product or service?
- **Need:** Do they have a clear problem your solution can solve?
- **Authority:** Can you reach key decision-makers?
- **Timing:** Are they ready to engage, or are they still in the research phase?

Sales Scenario Example:

The consultant researches the retail chain's recent expansion. Public records show a supply chain delay in its recent quarterly report. This indicates a clear operational need, suggesting a strong fit for the consultant's services.

Action Plan:

1. Use the BANT (Budget, Authority, Need, Timing) framework to qualify leads.
2. Conduct competitor and market analysis to understand client pain points.
3. Rank leads based on readiness, potential contract size, and revenue impact.

3. Develop – Build Relationships Through Engagement

With qualified leads in hand, the next step is Developing meaningful relationships. At this stage, your focus should be on nurturing the relationship through personalized engagement, trust-building, and ongoing value delivery.

Key Tactics:

- Personalize outreach by referencing the prospect's

specific needs.

- Schedule discovery calls, product demos, or personalized webinars.
- Share industry reports, research findings, or relevant case studies.
- Stay connected through consistent follow-ups.

Sales Scenario Example:

The consultant reaches out to the retail chain's operations manager with a personalized email highlighting the company's recent logistics challenges and offering a free consultation. After a successful initial meeting, they share a tailored proposal, demonstrating a clear understanding of the company's supply chain needs.

Action Plan:

1. Build rapport through personalized messaging and relevant content.
2. Host face-to-face meetings or video calls to build trust.
3. Provide value through free resources, consultations, or industry insights.

4. Recruit – Convert Prospects into Clients

The final stage is Recruiting, where you convert prospects into paying clients by securing a contract, partnership, or agreement. This involves negotiating terms, addressing objections, and ensuring a smooth onboarding process.

Key Tactics:

- Present tailored proposals addressing the prospect's specific needs.

- Offer clear pricing, terms, and service guarantees.

- Use testimonials, references, or case studies to reinforce credibility.

- Handle objections with confidence, providing data-driven responses.

Sales Scenario Example:

After multiple meetings and a strong value-focused proposal, the consultant finalizes a service contract with the retail chain, ensuring a six-month logistics optimization project. The onboarding process is seamless, setting the stage for future engagements.

Action Plan:

1. Schedule closing meetings or proposal reviews.

2. Use negotiation strategies that address the client's concerns while maintaining profitability.

3. Ensure a smooth transition from proposal acceptance to project implementation.

Applying the SADR Model in Sales

Step 1: Create a Sales Playbook

Document each phase of the SADR process in a structured sales playbook. Include criteria for spotting, assessing, developing, and recruiting leads.

Step 2: Build a Target Profile Template

Develop a target profile template that includes key details such as industry, annual revenue, challenges, and decision-making process.

Step 3: Execute Targeted Campaigns

Launch tailored campaigns based on your list of prioritized prospects. Ensure consistent follow-up and personalized engagement throughout the process.

Workshop
Activities

Activity 1: Lead Identification Exercise (Spot)

- **Objective:** Practice identifying potential leads using market research tools.

- **Instructions:**
  1. Provide participants with an industry report or dataset.
  2. Ask them to identify three promising leads based on specific criteria.
  3. Have each team present their leads and justify their selections.

Activity 2: Prospect Qualification Challenge (Assess)

- **Objective:** Qualify leads using the BANT framework.

- **Instructions:**
  1. Distribute several mock lead profiles.
  2. Ask teams to rank the leads using Budget, Authority, Need, and Timing.
  3. Discuss qualification decisions as a group.

Activity 3: Role-Playing Sales Engagement (Develop & Recruit)

- **Objective:** Practice pitching and closing deals using the SADR Model.

- **Instructions:**
  1. Pair participants into sellers and prospects.
  2. Each seller must use the SADR process to pitch their product or service.
  3. Prospects challenge the sellers with objections or concerns.
  4. Provide feedback on how well participants navigated the process.

F3EAD Cycle
(Operational Planning)

In the fast-paced world of sales, adaptability and precision are critical. Deals can be lost due to incomplete planning, slow responses, or missed opportunities. T o manage complex sales processes and ensure operational success, sales teams can adopt the F3EAD Cycle, a framework originating from military operations. This model—Find, Fix, Finish, Exploit, Analyze, Disseminate—offers a structured approach to problem-solving, negotiation, and project management.

By applying F3EAD, sales professionals can identify challenges, execute effective strategies, and continuously improve their processes based on real-world results. In this chapter, we'll explore how each phase of the F3EAD cycle can be adapted to the sales environment to close deals with precision and efficiency.

Breaking Down
the F3EAD Cycle

1. Find – Identify the Target or Problem

The first step in the F3EAD cycle is Find, which involves locating the target—in sales terms, identifying potential clients, problems, or opportunities. This includes researching leads, mapping the sales pipeline, and uncovering pain points through market research or client interactions.

Key Tactics:

- Conduct competitor and industry analysis.
- Use CRM tools to track leads and sales opportunities.
- Monitor client behavior and trigger events (e.g., business expansions or product launches).

Scenario Example:

An automotive supplier identifies a major car manufacturer looking for new component suppliers after a recent press release announcing a production expansion. This presents a valuable opportunity.

Action Plan:

- Use lead-generation tools and industry reports to identify prospects.
- Attend trade shows and events to spot emerging opportunities.
- Leverage sales intelligence tools to monitor key accounts and competitors.

2. Fix – Pinpoint and Define the Solution

Once a potential lead or problem is found, the next step is Fixing, which involves gathering more information, defining specific challenges, and planning a tailored approach. This includes determining decision-makers, understanding budget constraints, and creating a focused strategy to meet the prospect's specific needs.

Key Tactics:

- Conduct discovery calls or in-depth client interviews.

- Identify key stakeholders and decision-making structures.
- Build a clear picture of client needs, goals, and existing obstacles.

Scenario Example:

After an initial consultation, the automotive supplier discovers that the car manufacturer is experiencing delayed shipments from a current supplier, impacting its production schedule—a critical issue the supplier can address.

Action Plan:

- Conduct a detailed needs analysis through calls and questionnaires.
- Identify where your offering can provide the most immediate value.
- Develop a clear sales pitch targeting identified challenges.

3. Finish – Execute the Solution

With the problem clearly defined, the next step is Finishing, or taking action. This involves presenting tailored proposals, conducting negotiations, and closing the deal. The focus here is on precise execution with clearly defined goals and deadlines.

Key Tactics:

- Present customized sales proposals backed by data.
- Use sales scripts to handle objections effectively.
- Close deals using clear calls to action and contract agreements.

Scenario Example:

The automotive supplier delivers a proposal emphasizing its ability to offer faster shipping times, streamlined logistics, and guaranteed on-time deliveries. After several meetings and revisions, the contract is signed.

Action Plan:

- Schedule meetings with decision-makers for final presentations.
- Offer a clear value proposition with competitive terms.
- Close the deal by emphasizing urgency and reliability.

4. Exploit – Maximize the Opportunity

After closing the deal, the next step is Exploiting the win by delivering exceptional service and seeking additional business opportunities within the client's network. This includes cross-selling, upselling, and leveraging client referrals.

Key Tactics:

- Onboard the client with excellent service and support.
- Offer additional products or upgrades tailored to the client's evolving needs.
- Ask for client testimonials and referrals to build credibility.

Scenario Example:

The automotive supplier not only fulfills its first order but also suggests additional services, such as warehousing and inventory management. The client agrees, generating additional revenue streams.

Action Plan:

- Create personalized follow-up strategies for ongoing engagement.
- Offer promotional discounts on new services or products.
- Use client success stories as social proof in marketing campaigns.

5. Analyze – Review Performance and Results

No sales process is complete without Analyzing results. This involves reviewing key performance indicators (KPIs), measuring revenue gains, assessing client satisfaction, and identifying what worked and what didn't during the sales process.

Key Tactics:

- Conduct post-mortem reviews after major deals.
- Use CRM analytics and performance dashboards.
- Survey clients for feedback on service and product performance.

Scenario Example:

The automotive supplier holds a performance review after completing its first contract. Sales data shows that on-time deliveries increased production efficiency by 25%, exceeding client expectations.

Action Plan:

- Review internal sales metrics such as revenue growth and client retention.
- Conduct client satisfaction surveys.
- Identify gaps in service or missed upselling opportunities.

6. Disseminate – Share Lessons and Insights

The final step in the F3EAD cycle is Disseminating insights, meaning sharing lessons learned across the sales team. This ensures continuous improvement, better future pitches, and enhanced customer service strategies.

Key Tactics:

- Hold team debriefings or sales workshops.
- Create case studies and internal playbooks based on success stories.
- Share new tactics and strategies during team meetings.

Scenario Example:

The supplier's sales team holds a workshop reviewing the car manufacturer's account. They create a case study highlighting how the supplier solved logistical challenges, which becomes a key asset in future pitches.

Action Plan:

- Develop internal training sessions based on successful deals.
- Publish sales performance reports within the company.
- Update marketing collateral with new client success stories.

Workshop

Activities

Activity 1: Sales Process Simulation

- **Objective:** Practice applying the F3EAD cycle in a real-world sales scenario.

- **Instructions:**
  1. Divide participants into sales teams.
  2. Assign each team a hypothetical client with specific needs.
  3. Teams must navigate the F3EAD cycle from "Find" to "Disseminate."
  4. Teams present their outcomes and lessons learned.

Activity 2: Deal Post-Mortem Review

- **Objective:** Conduct a deal review using the F3EAD model.
- **Instructions:**
  1. Select a recently closed (or lost) deal.
  2. Walk through each phase of the F3EAD cycle.
  3. Identify what went well and what could be improved.
  4. Discuss how lessons learned can be applied to future sales processes.

Activity 3: Client Engagement Plan

- **Objective:** Build a client engagement strategy using the F3EAD model.

- **Instructions:**
  1. Assign participants a fictional client with detailed needs.
  2. Teams must create a full engagement plan covering all F3EAD steps.
  3. Present the strategy for group feedback and adjustments.

The KGB's "Four Ds"
(Psychological Manipulation)

Negotiation is a battlefield where control of the conversation determines victory. While direct tactics can be easily identified, subtle psychological maneuvers often go unnoticed, allowing the skilled negotiator to guide outcomes effectively. The KGB's "Four Ds" Framework—Deny, Disrupt, Degrade, and Deceive—was developed as a set of psychological tactics for managing and controlling adversarial situations. In sales negotiations, these methods can be applied ethically to navigate difficult interactions, regain control, and secure desired outcomes.

While manipulation may seem like a harsh term, in sales, ethical influence is essential. Knowing how to apply these tactics can help counter aggressive negotiations, break through deadlocks, and realign conversations toward productive outcomes—all while maintaining professional integrity.

Breaking Down
the "Four Ds" Framework

1. Deny – Block or Refute Unwanted Assertions

Definition: To Deny means to refute claims, reject demands, or block unwanted questions and assertions to regain control of a conversation. This tactic prevents the opposing party from gaining an advantage by putting you on the defensive.

When to Use It:

- When facing unfair accusations or mischaracterizations.
- When asked for sensitive information you're not ready to disclose.
- When competitors' false claims are brought up by the client.

Sales Scenario Example:

During a contract negotiation, a procurement officer falsely claims that a competitor is offering better terms. The salesperson denies the claim by referencing industry-standard pricing and past client testimonials, redirecting the conversation toward the unique value of their offer.

How to Apply:

- Stay calm and composed; never become defensive.
- Deny false claims with factual corrections, using data or testimonials.
- Use firm, clear language like: *"That's not accurate. Let me clarify..."*

2. Disrupt – Create Controlled Chaos

Definition: To Disrupt means to intentionally create a moment of confusion or distraction to break the opponent's flow and reset the conversation on your terms. Disruption can be as simple as changing the subject or introducing unexpected information.

When to Use It:

- When the negotiation becomes adversarial or stuck.
- When the client is hyper-focused on a single objection.
- When controlling the agenda is essential.

Sales Scenario Example:

During a budget negotiation that's going nowhere, a salesperson disrupts the conversation by introducing a limited-time promotion. This shift in focus breaks the deadlock, prompting the client to reconsider the offer more urgently.

How to Apply:

- Change the subject by introducing new information.

- Shift focus to another product feature, benefit, or limited-time offer.

- Ask an unrelated but strategic question to regain attention and control.

3. Degrade – Weaken Opposition Arguments

Definition: To Degrade means to subtly weaken or undermine the credibility of the other party's arguments, data, or position. This tactic works by exposing flaws, inconsistencies, or weaknesses in the opponent's stance.

When to Use It:

- When the client insists on incorrect data or assumptions.

- When the competition's proposal contains errors.

- When false information is being used as leverage.

Sales Scenario Example:

A prospect claims a competitor offers superior after-sales service. The salesperson degrades this claim by highlighting the competitor's customer service rating on third-party review sites, showing poor responsiveness in past dealings.

How to Apply:

- Use precise, factual language to highlight inconsistencies.
- Present third-party validation, industry benchmarks, or testimonials.
- Avoid direct attacks—focus on the facts and let the evidence speak for itself.

4. Deceive – Use Misdirection (Ethically)

Definition: Deceive involves using strategic misdirection to guide the opponent toward a desired conclusion without revealing your full hand. In sales, this can mean managing expectations or withholding certain details until the right time.

When to Use It:

- When revealing too much information could jeopardize the deal.
- When creating perceived value through controlled information release.
- When steering a negotiation toward favorable terms.

Sales Scenario Example:

A software vendor withholds details about additional premium features until the client is already leaning toward purchasing the base product. Once interest is secured, the vendor introduces the premium features as value-added options to upsell.

How to Apply:

- Use controlled information disclosure to maintain leverage.

- Frame your offering as a "hidden value" revealed at the right moment.
- Stay truthful, ensuring that all disclosed information is accurate.

Applying the "Four Ds" in Sales Negotiations

1. Recognize When to Use Them:

Monitor the flow of the conversation. If the discussion becomes adversarial, manipulative, or deadlocked, consider using one of the Four Ds.

2. Choose the Right Tactic:

- Use Deny to counter false claims or accusations.
- Use Disrupt to break a negative negotiation cycle or create urgency.
- Use Degrade to challenge weak competitor claims.
- Use Deceive (ethically) by controlling the timing of information release.

3. Maintain Ethical Standards:

- Use these tactics only when necessary and always truthfully.
- Avoid manipulative practices that could harm long-term relationships.

During a critical contract renewal, a senior sales executive is negotiating with a major corporate client who insists on a steep discount, claiming a competitor offers better terms. Application of the Four Ds:

1. **Deny:** The executive confidently denies the competitor's claim by referencing verified client success stories.

2. **Disrupt:** When the client fixates on price, the executive disrupts the conversation by highlighting limited-time implementation support and a future upgrade path.

3. **Degrade:** The executive references independent industry ratings showing the competitor's poor after-sales service.

4. **Deceive:** At a key moment, the executive reveals an exclusive bundled service that wasn't discussed earlier, tipping the scales in their favor.

Result: The client sees the greater long-term value of staying with the current vendor and signs the renewal contract.

Workshop

Activities

Activity 1: Negotiation Role-Play

- **Objective:** Practice applying the Four Ds in a live negotiation.

- **Instructions:**

  1. Divide participants into pairs–one playing the salesperson and the other a difficult client.

  2. The salesperson must use at least two "D" tactics to steer the conversation.

  3. Reverse roles and provide feedback on negotiation tactics used.

Activity 2: Case Study Breakdown

- **Objective:** Analyze real-world sales negotiations through the Four Ds framework.

- **Instructions:**

  1. Present a real or hypothetical negotiation case.

  2. Have teams identify where each of the Four Ds could have been applied for a better outcome.

  3. Discuss results and alternative tactics.

Activity 3: Real Deal Analysis

- **Objective:** Review past sales deals and evaluate where the Four Ds could have been applied.

- **Instructions:**

  1. Sales teams choose a past negotiation from their records.

  2. They analyze each stage of the negotiation and discuss missed opportunities for applying the Four Ds.

  3. Teams present lessons learned.

SARA Model
(Behavioral Change and Influence)

The ability to adapt to changing markets, customer preferences, and industry trends is the hallmark of a successful sales professional. The SARA Model—an acronym for Scan, Analyze, Respond, and Assess—is a dynamic problem-solving and influence framework designed to identify opportunities, adapt offerings, and drive continuous improvement. Originating from behavioral science and operational planning, SARA provides a systematic approach to achieving sales growth and improving customer engagement.

This chapter explores how the SARA Model works, its application in sales, and how you can use it to proactively adjust to shifting market conditions and buyer behavior.

Breaking Down
the SARA Model

1. Scan – Identify Environmental Trends and Market Signals

Definition: Scanning involves observing the external environment to identify emerging trends, industry developments, and potential sales opportunities. This process requires gathering relevant market intelligence, monitoring customer behavior, and staying ahead of competitors.

Sales Questions:

- What are the current industry trends affecting customer behavior?
- What new products or services are competitors launching?
- What external factors (economic shifts, regulations) could impact our sales process?

Scenario Example:

A health insurance company notices a growing trend of young professionals opting for flexible, customizable insurance plans due to changing employment patterns. This insight is gathered through social media monitoring, industry reports, and feedback from recent inquiries.

Action Plan:

1. Use market research tools to track trends.
2. Monitor competitors' offerings and promotional campaigns.
3. Follow industry news, customer reviews, and social media conversations.

2. Analyze – Evaluate Data and Identify Key Opportunities

Definition: Analyzing involves evaluating data collected during the scanning phase to uncover key insights. This step helps sales teams determine where to focus their efforts and prioritize opportunities that align with business goals.

Sales Questions:

- What unmet customer needs have been identified?
- Where are we losing potential clients in the sales funnel?
- Which customer segments offer the greatest revenue potential?

Scenario Example:

The health insurance company discovers that while young professionals are interested in flexible plans, most feel overwhelmed by the application process. Analytics from their website show a high drop-off rate during the registration phase. This signals an opportunity to simplify and streamline the process.

Action Plan:

1. Use CRM data and website analytics to track customer behavior.

2. Identify common objections and purchasing barriers from sales call records.

3. Map out customer journeys to pinpoint potential drop-off points.

3. Respond – Take Action with Targeted Strategies

Definition: Responding involves developing and implementing targeted solutions based on insights gained during the analysis phase. This step turns data-driven findings into tailored sales strategies, marketing campaigns, and product adjustments.

Sales Questions:

- What specific actions will address the identified needs?

- How can we personalize our outreach based on customer behavior?

- What resources and teams are needed to execute the response plan?

■ **Scenario Example:**

To reduce customer drop-offs, the health insurance company introduces a new feature: "Quick Quote," a simplified enrollment process offering instant coverage estimates. The team also launches a social media campaign showcasing how easy it is to sign up, using testimonials from satisfied customers.

Action Plan:

1. Develop personalized marketing campaigns based on identified customer pain points.
2. Launch product enhancements or service improvements.
3. Train the sales team on the new approach to ensure consistent messaging.

4. Assess – Measure Results and Refine Strategies

Definition: Assessing involves reviewing and evaluating the results of the implemented actions. This step ensures that the applied strategies are effective and provides an opportunity to refine or adjust tactics for better performance in the future.

Sales Questions:

- Did the new strategy improve customer acquisition or retention?
- Which metrics showed the most improvement, and which areas still need work?
- What lessons can be applied to future campaigns?

Scenario Example:

After launching the new enrollment feature and marketing campaign, the health insurance company sees a 40% increase in customer sign-ups. Customer feedback highlights that the simplified process made purchasing insurance far easier. The company refines the process further by adding a live chat feature to answer common questions in real time.

Action Plan:

1. Measure campaign results using KPIs like sales growth, customer satisfaction scores, and sign-up rates.

2. Conduct post-campaign reviews with key sales and marketing team members.

3. Adjust tactics based on performance metrics and customer feedback.

Applying the SARA Model in Sales

Step 1: Build a Market Intelligence Dashboard

Create a centralized dashboard using CRM, sales analytics, and third-party tools to collect and organize industry data, sales performance metrics, and customer insights.

Step 2: Conduct Monthly Market Scans

Schedule regular team reviews of market trends, sales data, and customer feedback to ensure that emerging opportunities and threats are identified early.

Step 3: Implement Adaptive Sales Strategies

Based on insights gained through scanning and analysis, launch targeted campaigns or product enhancements quickly and efficiently.

Step 4: Hold Quarterly Reviews

Host quarterly assessment meetings to review completed campaigns, compare results to benchmarks, and adjust future sales strategies accordingly.

Scenario in Action:

The Health Insurance Sales Team

During a quarterly strategy meeting, the health insurance sales team applies the SARA Model to increase enrollment among young professionals:

- **Scan:** They monitor industry trends showing that young professionals prefer flexible insurance plans.

- **Analyze:** Data shows that most prospects abandon the sign-up process halfway due to its complexity.

- **Respond:** They introduce a "Quick Quote" feature, simplifying the registration process.

- **Assess:** After implementing the change, customer acquisition rates increase by 40%, leading to record-breaking sales performance.

Workshop

Activities

Activity 1: Market Trend Scanning
- **Objective:** Practice scanning the market for emerging opportunities.

- **Instructions:**
    1. Provide industry-specific reports and news articles.
    2. Ask participants to identify three potential sales opportunities.
    3. Teams present findings, explaining why the identified trends matter.

Activity 2: Data Analysis Challenge

- **Objective:** Evaluate customer data to uncover actionable insights.

- **Instructions:**
    1. Provide fictional sales data (e.g., CRM reports, web analytics).
    2. Teams analyze the data to identify sales bottlenecks and areas for improvement.
    3. Each team presents its findings and suggests strategies.

Activity 3: Response Strategy Development

- **Objective:** Create a customer-focused sales strategy using the SARA model.

- **Instructions:**
    1. Assign teams a fictional client with specific needs.
    2. Teams must create a full engagement plan using Scan, Analyze, Respond, and Assess steps.
    3. Present the strategy for group feedback.

REACT Model
(Crisis Management and Persuasion)

In the fast-moving world of sales, crises are inevitable—whether it's a major product recall, a dissatisfied client, or a sudden market shift. What separates successful sales professionals from the rest is their ability to handle such challenges swiftly, strategically, and decisively. The REACT Model, originally developed for crisis management, provides a step-by-step framework to navigate high-stakes situations. It stands for Recognize, Evaluate, Act, Communicate, and Time—each stage crucial for resolving issues while maintaining trust and credibility.

This chapter explores how to apply the REACT Model to critical sales negotiations, customer service problems, and internal business crises. By mastering this framework, you'll be prepared to manage even the most challenging situations with confidence and control.

Breaking Down
the REACT Model

1. Recognize – Identify Early Warning Signs

Definition: The first step in crisis management is recognizing that a problem exists. In sales, this means detecting early warning signs such as negative customer feedback, delayed shipments, or stalled negotiations before they escalate into full-blown crises.

Sales Questions:

- Are clients raising repeated concerns or objections?

- Is customer satisfaction declining based on survey results or reviews?

- Are there signs of budget cuts, canceled meetings, or missed deadlines?

▌ Scenario Example:

A sales manager at a tech company notices that several major clients have been expressing dissatisfaction with product delivery timelines. Recognizing this as an early warning sign, she initiates a review of the logistics process.

Action Plan:

- Monitor customer communications regularly (emails, calls, reviews).

- Set up alerts for negative social media mentions.

- Establish a process for frontline sales staff to escalate potential issues.

2. Evaluate – Assess the Situation and Options

Definition: Once a crisis has been identified, the next step is to evaluate the severity of the issue and potential solutions. This involves gathering relevant information, determining the scope of the problem, and assessing available resources to resolve it.

Sales Questions:

- How serious is the issue? Is it local, regional, or company-wide?

- What is the potential impact on revenue, reputation, and customer relationships?

- What resources and team members are needed to address the issue?

Scenario Example:

The tech sales manager gathers data from the logistics team and discovers that a third-party supplier is causing delays. She evaluates whether switching to an alternative supplier or renegotiating delivery terms would minimize downtime.

Action Plan:

- Conduct a quick but thorough assessment of the problem's root cause.

- Gather input from relevant teams such as logistics, customer support, and sales.

- Prioritize solutions based on impact, cost, and speed of implementation.

3. Act – Take Decisive Action

Definition: Once options have been evaluated, decisive action must be taken. Delays can worsen the situation, so swift and confident decision-making is critical. Even if the solution is temporary, acting quickly shows commitment and responsiveness.

Sales Questions:

- What immediate actions can be taken to prevent the issue from worsening?

- Which team members will be responsible for executing the action plan?

- Are backup plans ready in case the first solution fails?

Scenario Example:

The sales manager instructs the logistics team to switch to a faster shipping provider temporarily while renegotiating a long-term contract with the current supplier. She also informs key clients that their orders will be prioritized for immediate dispatch.

Action Plan:

- Designate a task force or response team.
- Take immediate steps to stabilize the situation.
- Document actions taken for future review and learning.

4. Communicate – Keep Stakeholders Informed

Definition: Communication is the cornerstone of effective crisis management. Regular updates–both internal and external–are essential to managing expectations and preserving trust. Clear, transparent communication can prevent misunderstandings and mitigate negative reactions.

Sales Questions:

- Who needs to be informed–clients, internal teams, or external partners?
- What key messages should be conveyed?
- How frequently should updates be provided?

Scenario Example:

The sales manager issues an email update to affected clients, explaining the delay and outlining the immediate steps being taken. She also holds a team-wide briefing to align internal staff on the situation and provide talking points for client interactions.

Action Plan:

- Create a central communication hub for updates and FAQs.
- Use a consistent and transparent tone.
- Provide regular updates until the crisis is fully resolved.

5. Time – Manage the Clock for Effective Resolution

Definition: Timing is critical in both managing and resolving crises. Delaying action can cause damage, while rushing without adequate preparation can backfire. Balancing urgency with strategic planning ensures that actions are both timely and effective.

Sales Questions:

- How urgent is the issue, and what deadlines must be met?
- Are key stakeholders available to assist with resolution efforts?
- What milestones should be tracked to measure progress?

Scenario Example:

The sales manager sets a 72-hour deadline for the logistics team to secure a new supplier while maintaining direct communication with affected clients. Regular check-ins ensure that the timeline stays on track.

Action Plan:

- Set clear deadlines for response and resolution efforts.
- Track progress through daily or weekly check-ins.
- Adjust timelines based on real-time developments.

Applying the REACT Model in Sales

Step 1: Establish a Crisis Response Team

Assign key team members specific roles, such as communication lead, logistics manager, and customer service coordinator.

Step 2: Develop a Crisis Playbook

Create a crisis management playbook that outlines common scenarios and pre-approved response strategies based on the REACT Model.

Step 3: Conduct Regular Simulations

Hold regular crisis response simulations to test team readiness and refine the crisis management process.

Scenario in Action: The Product Recall Crisis

A health-tech company faces a product recall after discovering a minor defect in its wearable devices. The sales manager leads the team through the REACT Model process:

1. **Recognize:** The sales team notices an increase in customer complaints about defective devices.

2. **Evaluate:** The product recall affects 5% of current orders but risks growing into a full-blown PR crisis.

3. **Act:** The company recalls all affected devices, offering free replacements and extended warranties.

4. **Communicate:** Regular updates are sent to affected customers and sales teams, explaining the recall process.

5. **Time:** The team sets a 30-day deadline for completing the recall and offering replacements.

Workshop
Activities

Activity 1: Crisis Role-Play Simulation

- **Objective:** Practice managing a crisis using the REACT Model.

- **Instructions:**
  1. Divide participants into teams and assign a crisis scenario (e.g., a delayed product launch or product defect).
  2. 2. 3. T eams must apply each step of the REACT Model to manage the situation.
  3. T eams present their response plans for group feedback.

Activity 2: Real-World Case Study Analysis

- **Objective:** Learn from real-world crisis management examples.

- **Instructions:**
  1. Present a real-world sales or product recall case study.
  2. Ask teams to identify how the REACT Model could have been applied.
  3. Discuss potential alternative responses and lessons learned.

Activity 3: Build a Crisis Playbook

- **Objective:** Create a personalized crisis management plan.
- **Instructions:**
  1. Have teams create a sales-specific crisis management playbook using the REACT framework.
  2. Include key roles, timelines, and communication templates.

Conclusion

This chapter illustrates the power of spycraft models in sales, providing a strategic lens to understand and leverage human motivations effectively. By adopting espionage techniques such as the MICE framework and the CARVER Matrix, sales professionals can prioritize and engage targets with a precision that significantly enhances their influence and success rates in any negotiation scenario.

CHAPTER 29

Personality Decoding – Psychological Assessments in Sales

"

Decoding personalities is not just about understanding who stands before you, but about adapting your strategy to resonate deeply with their core, transforming prospects into partners.

"

Understanding the personalities of both clients and sales personnel can significantly increase the efficacy of sales strategies. This chapter delves into various personality assessment tools, providing insights into how these frameworks can be leveraged in the context of sales.

1. The Four Temperaments (Ancient Personality Test)

Basic Overview: One of the oldest personality frameworks, the Four T emperaments categorize individuals as Sanguine, Phlegmatic, Choleric, or Melancholic, each associated with specific personality traits.

Introduction Story: A sales manager uses the Four Temperaments to form balanced sales teams that play to each member's strengths.

- **Sales Application:** Understanding a prospect's temperament can guide the tone and approach of sales pitches, such as using energetic presentations for Sanguine individuals or detailed data for Melancholic prospects.

- **Case Study:** A car dealership implemented temperament-based training for their sales staff, resulting in a 20% increase in customer satisfaction and sales.

Categories:

- Sanguine (Social & Optimistic): Energetic, enthusiastic, loves people.
- Choleric (Assertive & Goal-Driven): Ambitious, direct, and action-oriented.
- Melancholic (Analytical & Detail-Oriented): Thoughtful, reserved, prefers precision.
- Phlegmatic (Calm & Supportive): Laid-back, empathetic, and conflict-averse.

How to Use:

- Ask the person how they handle stressful situations, teamwork, or decision-making.

- Look for energy levels, focus on results vs. people, and responsiveness to change.

Sales or Business Insight:

- Sanguine people respond well to fun, engaging pitches.
- Choleric types appreciate directness and efficiency.
- Melancholic individuals prefer data-backed reasoning.
- Phlegmatic personalities value stability and long-term relationships.

2. DISC Personality Profile

Basic Overview: DISC measures dominance, influence, steadiness, and conscientiousness, helping predict behavior towards others and the daily response to tasks and challenges.

Introduction Story: A real estate agent tailors her approach based on DISC profiles to better connect with potential buyers.

- **Sales Application:** Using DISC to tailor communication styles can enhance client relations and improve negotiation outcomes.

- **Case Study:** A software company used DISC profiles to customize sales presentations, leading to a 30% improvement in closing rates.

Categories:

- **Dominance (D):** Focus on results and action.
- **Influence (I):** Focus on relationships and persuasion.
- **Steadiness (S):** Focus on stability and support.
- **Conscientiousness (C):** Focus on accuracy and structure.

How to Use:

Observe how someone communicates:

- Are they direct and assertive (D) or friendly and talkative (I)?
- Are they calm and steady (S) or precise and detail-oriented (C)?

Quick Test Question:

"If you were leading a project team, how would you handle team conflict?"

- **D:** Resolve it quickly and make a decision.
- **I:** Mediate with empathy and create harmony.
- **S:** Avoid conflict and focus on team stability.
- **C:** Analyze the root cause and propose a structured solution.

Sales Insight:

- Dominant types like competitive, results-driven deals.
- Influencers appreciate people-focused pitches with personal stories.
- Steady personalities want long-term guarantees.
- Conscientious types need detailed proposals and precise numbers.

3. The Big Five Personality Traits (OCEAN)

Basic Overview: This model assesses individuals across five dimensions: Openness, Conscientiousness, Extraversion, Agreeableness, and Neuroticism.

Introduction Story: A marketing team uses OCEAN traits to segment their audience and create targeted advertising campaigns.

Framework Breakdown:

- **Sales Application:** Recognizing these traits helps salespeople predict client needs and customize their sales strategies accordingly.

- **Case Study:** A financial services firm tailored their client interactions based on OCEAN profiles, which significantly reduced client turnover.

The Big Five assesses five universal traits that predict how people behave:

- **Openness:** Creative and curious vs. conservative and routine-oriented.

- **Conscientiousness:** Organized and responsible vs. spontaneous and careless.

- **Extraversion:** Outgoing and social vs. introverted and reserved.

- **Agreeableness:** Cooperative and empathetic vs. competitive and challenging.

- **Neuroticism:** Emotionally reactive vs. calm and stable.

How to Use:

Ask casual questions:

- *"How do you approach new challenges at work?"* (Openness)
- *"Do you prefer to plan every detail or adapt on the fly?"* (Conscientiousness)
- *"How do you relax after work?"* (Extraversion)
- *"How do you resolve disagreements?"* (Agreeableness)
- *"How do you handle stress under pressure?"* (Neuroticism)

Sales Insight:

- **High openness** = interested in innovative, future-focused solutions.
- **High conscientiousness** = wants reliable, well-structured offers.
- **High extraversion** = enjoys engaging, energetic presentations.
- **High agreeableness** = responds well to collaborative pitches.
- **Low neuroticism** = prefers high-stakes, results-driven environments.

4. Cognitive Motivators
(Based on MICE Framework)

Basic Overview: This approach adapts the MICE framework (Money, Ideology, Coercion, Ego) from intelligence operations to understand what drives a person's decisions.

Introduction Story: An investment broker uses cognitive motivators to craft compelling investment proposals.

Framework Breakdown:

- **Sales Application:** Identifying a client's primary motivators can guide the development of more persuasive and relevant sales pitches.

- **Case Study:** A luxury goods retailer increased upselling by training their staff to identify and appeal to the dominant motivators of their customers.

The CIA's MICE (Money, Ideology, Coercion, Ego) can be adapted into simple motivator questions to assess what drives someone.

How to Use:

- **Ask:** "What motivates you most in your career or personal goals?"

- **Interpret Answers:**

  » **Money:** Seeks financial rewards, bonuses, and raises.

  » **Ideology:** Motivated by purpose, social good, or mission-driven work.

  » **Coercion (Security):** Motivated by avoiding risks, penalties, or losing something valuable.

  » **Ego:** Craves recognition, status, and prestige.

Sales Insight:

Frame proposals around the identified motivator: money (ROI), ideology (impact), security (reliability), or ego (exclusive recognition).

5. MBTI (Myers-Briggs Type Indicator) Shortcut

Basic Overview: MBTI categorizes individuals into 16 different personality types based on four dichotomies: Introversion/Extraversion, Sensing/Intuition, Thinking/Feeling, Judging/Perceiving.

Introduction Story: A project manager uses MBTI shortcuts to better understand project stakeholders and tailor project communications.

Framework Breakdown:

- **Sales Application:** MBTI helps in predicting client preferences and improving team dynamics within sales teams.

- **Case Study:** A consulting firm applied MBTI assessments to streamline team assignments, enhancing project outcomes and client satisfaction.

While the full MBTI has 16 personality types, you can assess using four binary preferences:

- **Introversion (I) vs. Extraversion (E):** Social energy.

- **Sensing (S) vs. Intuition (N):** Focus on details vs. big-picture ideas.

- **Thinking (T) vs. Feeling (F):** Logic-driven vs. emotion-driven decisions.

- **Judging (J) vs. Perceiving (P):** Structured/planned vs. flexible/spontaneous.

How to Use:

- **Ask:** *"How do you prefer to work on projects: planned or adaptable?"* (J vs. P)

- **Ask:** *"Do you decide based on data or personal values?"* (T vs. F)

Sales Insight:

- I vs. E affects how much interaction they want in a sales process.

- S vs. N impacts how much detail they need to feel comfortable.

- T vs. F determines whether logic or emotion will close the deal.

- J vs. P predicts if they want structured timelines or flexible solutions.

6. The Enneagram (Motivational Core Types)

Basic Overview: The Enneagram describes nine personality types based on core motivations, fears, and desires, offering deep insights into behavioral patterns.

Introduction Story: A sales leader uses the Enneagram to coach her team on handling various types of client interactions.

Framework Breakdown:

- **Sales Application:** Understanding the core motivations of clients and colleagues can significantly enhance interpersonal effectiveness and sales success.

- **Case Study:** A health club personalized their membership sales strategies based on the Enneagram types of prospective members, boosting retention by 25%.

The Enneagram categorizes people into nine types based on their core motivations. You can informally assess these through casual conversation:

1. **Reformer (Perfectionist)**– Motivated by doing the right thing.

2. **Helper (Giver)**– Motivated by helping others.

3. **Achiever (Success-Driven)**– Motivated by success and admiration.

4. **Individualist (Creative)**– Motivated by self-expression.

5. **Investigator (Thinker)**– Motivated by understanding and knowledge.

6. **Loyalist (Security-Seeker)**– Motivated by safety and support.

7. **Enthusiast (Adventure-Seeker)**– Motivated by excitement and experience.

8. **Challenger (Leader)**– Motivated by control and power.

9. **Peacemaker (Mediator)**– Motivated by harmony and conflict resolution.

How to Use:

Ask: *"What drives you the most in your personal and professional life?"* Look for themes like success, stability, or creativity in their response.

Workshop

Activities

To solidify the application of these personality assessment tools in sales, the following activities are suggested:

1. **Personality Role-Playing:** Participants adopt different personality profiles and engage in sales scenarios to observe how various approaches affect outcomes.

2. **Group Analysis:** T eams work together to assess the personality profiles of case studies or real clients and plan tailored sales strategies.

3. **Personality Mapping:** Sales teams map their own personalities and discuss how their strengths and weaknesses affect their sales techniques.

4. **Client Simulation Exercises:** T eams use personality insights to prep re and execute pitches to simulated clients with known personality types.

Quick Conversation Starters for Informal Assessment

1. *"What type of work environment do you thrive in?"* (Leadership style, collaboration preference)

2. *"How do you typically make big decisions— quickly or after careful thought?"* (Risk tolerance, decisiveness)

3. *"What's been your biggest career success and how did you achieve it?"* (Motivation, work ethic)

4. *"What keeps you motivated when things get tough?"* (Resilience, long-term vision)

5. *"How do you handle conflicts at work?"* (Problem-solving style, diplomacy)

These activities are designed to make the theoretical aspects of personality assessments practical and actionable, enabling sales professionals to use psychological insights to enhance their effectiveness and achieve greater success.

Conclusion

Understanding the psychological underpinnings of different personality types enables sales professionals to tailor their approaches for maximum resonance and effectiveness. Tools like DISC, the Big Five, and the Enneagram are more than just theoretical concepts; they are practical instruments that transform every sales interaction into a customized engagement, enhancing the potential for successful outcomes.

CHAPTER 30

Emotional Warfare – Managing Your Own Emotions Under Fire

"

In the heat of negotiation, the ability to manage your emotions is your greatest shield and your opponent's greatest mystery.

"

Navigating emotional landscapes skillfully is crucial in high-stakes sales environments. This chapter addresses strategies for recognizing, controlling, and channeling emotions to maintain professionalism and effectiveness in challenging situations.

1. Recognize Early Signs of Anger (Self-Awareness)

Introduction: Early recognition of anger allows for timely intervention, preventing escalation and preserving relationships.

Overview: Understanding physical cues (tense muscles, clenched jaws) and emotional symptoms (irritation, impatience) can signal the onset of anger.

Case Study: A sales manager noticed these early signs during a team meeting and took a short break, which helped defuse potential conflicts and refocused the team on the agenda.

The first step is recognizing when you're getting angry before it takes control. The body gives clear **early warning signs** of emotional escalation:

Physical Cues:

- Increased heart rate (fight-or-flight response)
- Tensed muscles (clenched jaw or fists)
- Shallow or faster breathing

Mental Cues:

- Negative self-talk (*"I can't believe they said that!"*)
- Mental rehearsing of how you'll "respond aggressively"
- Black-and-white thinking (*"They're being completely unreasonable!"*)

Control Strategy:

- **Check-In Question:** *"What am I feeling right now? What's causing this reaction?"*

- **Tactical Pause:** Take a controlled breath (inhale for 4 seconds, hold for 2, exhale for 6). This resets the nervous system.

2. Prevent Others from Getting to You (Mental Deflection)

Introduction: Mental deflection involves maintaining a psychological barrier that prevents others' negative emotions from affecting you.

Overview: Techniques include visualizing a physical shield, focusing on factual communication, and maintaining empathy without emotional involvement.

Case Study: In a heated negotiation, a salesperson used mental deflection to stay calm when the client became verbally aggressive, which eventually led to a successful deal closure without personal conflict.

Some people intentionally push emotional buttons to destabilize you. Use these techniques to prevent being manipulated:

- **Label the Behavior:** Silently acknowledge, *"They're trying to provoke me."* Recognizing manipulation helps detach emotionally.

- **Create Emotional Distance:** Pretend you're watching the interaction as a third-party observer. This helps reduce emotional involvement.

- **Silent Counter-Narrative:** Use a mental mantra like *"Stay calm. This is a game. I control my reaction."*

3. Emotional Reframing (Mental Reset)

Introduction: Emotional reframing involves changing your perspective on a situation to alter its emotional impact.

Overview: This might mean viewing a tense negotiation as a challenge rather than a threat, thus transforming anxiety into excitement and focus.

Case Study: A pharmaceutical rep reframed a series of rejections not as failures but as steps towards finding the right approach, which improved her resilience and sales performance.

Reframing is the skill of changing how you interpret a negative experience, reducing emotional intensity.

How to Reframe:

- From Personal to Neutral:
  - » **Instead of:** *"They're insulting me!"*
  - » **Reframe:** *"They're projecting frustration or insecurity. It's not about me."*
- From Threat to Opportunity:
  - » **Instead of:** *"I'm being attacked."*
  - » **Reframe:** *"This is my chance to demonstrate control and composure."*

4. Stay Cool in the Moment (Crisis Control)

Introduction: Immediate control of emotions is essential in unexpected high-pressure situations.

Overview: Techniques include deep breathing, pausing before responding, and using neutral language.

Case Study: During a critical sales pitch, the lead salesperson remained composed under pressure by focusing on slow, steady breathing and concise, clear responses, successfully navigating the team through a tough Q&A session.

Use tactical conversation control when someone is trying to provoke you:

Verbal De-escalation Tactics:

- **Stay Calm and Speak Softly:** Reduces tension. The louder they get, the softer you respond.

- **Ask Clarifying Questions:** Shifts focus from emotions to facts. Example:
  - » *"Help me understand what you need from me right now."*
  - » *"What can we do to resolve this issue?"*

Avoid Emotional Traps:

- **Avoid Defensiveness:** Don't justify or explain yourself unnecessarily. Stay focused on the issue.

- **Ignore Personal Attacks:** Respond only to the relevant business points.

5. Long-Term Anger Management Strategies (Emotional Mastery)

Introduction: Long-term strategies involve developing habits that reduce the overall incidence and intensity of anger.

Detailed Overview: Regular exercise, meditation, journaling, and professional counseling are effective methods.

Case Study: A senior negotiator incorporated yoga and mindfulness into his routine, significantly reducing his stress levels and improving his negotiation outcomes.

Build Emotional Intelligence (EQ):

- **Self-Awareness:** Journal your triggers and responses to recognize patterns.

- **Self-Regulation:** Practice calming techniques daily (mindfulness or meditation).

- **Empathy Training:** Imagine the situation from the other person's perspective to reduce resentment.

Use the "10-Second Rule":

Count silently to 10 before responding to provocative comments. This small delay reduces impulsive reactions.

Controlled Exposure (Stress Simulation):

Regularly practice staying calm in stressful simulated environments (role-plays, negotiations). The more accustomed you are to pressure, the less reactive you'll be in real scenarios.

6. Mental Models for Staying in Control

Introduction: Mental models are frameworks that help maintain emotional control through structured thinking and behavior patterns.

Detailed Overview: Models such as "OODA Loop" (observe, orient, decide, act) can help maintain clarity and calm in stressful situations.

Case Study: A sales director used the OODA Loop during a complex merger discussion to continuously adjust her strategies based on the evolving dynamics, ensuring her team stayed on track and reacted promptly to changes. Other strategies to try out are:

The "Gray Man" Strategy:

- Act neutral, calm, and emotionally detached—like a "gray man" who blends into the background without reacting emotionally.

The Samurai Mindset (Stoicism):

- **Key Principle:** You can't control what happens, but you can control your reaction.

- **Mantra:** *"I remain calm because I choose how I respond."* So, never respond emotionally, only strategically.

The "Chess Master" Mentality:

- Visualize the entire situation like a chessboard. Think several moves ahead rather than reacting impulsively.

The Tactical Pause (Breathing Method):

- **Box Breathing Technique:** Inhale for 4 seconds, hold for 4 seconds, exhale for 4 seconds, hold for 4 seconds. This resets your body's stress response in 30 seconds.

Real-World Case Example: Business Negotiation A detailed example could involve a sales executive who uses all these emotional management techniques to secure a critical deal with a difficult client, illustrating the application of each strategy throughout different phases of the negotiation.

Workshop Activities

To embed these emotional management skills, the following workshop activities can be implemented:

- **Role-Playing Scenarios:** Participants practice recognizing signs of anger and employing deflection and reframing techniques in simulated sales scenarios.

- **Group Discussions:** Teams discuss real-life situations where emotional management made a difference in sales outcomes.

- **Breathing Exercises:** A coach leads exercises in breathing and mindfulness to demonstrate how to regain emotional control.

- **Emotional Resilience Challenges:** Participants share personal triggers and collaboratively develop personalized management strategies.

These activities help participants internalize the techniques discussed in the chapter, ensuring they are prepared to handle emotional challenges effectively in their sales careers.

Conclusion

The ability to manage and control one's emotions in high-stress sales situations is a critical determinant of success. The techniques discussed—ranging from recognizing early signs of emotional distress to employing tactical pauses—equip sales professionals with the tools to remain composed and focused, turning potential conflicts into opportunities for strategic advantage.

CHAPTER 31

Psychological Armor – Defense Against Manipulation

"

Building your psychological armor in sales isn't just about resisting manipulation, it's about crafting a mindset that turns deceit into opportunities for reinforcement and growth.

"

In the complex world of sales, manipulation tactics can often undermine a professional's confidence and effectiveness. This chapter equips salespeople with the tools to identify and counteract various manipulative behaviors, fostering a robust psychological defense that enhances both personal resilience and negotiation success.

Recognizing Psychological Manipulation Tactics Used in Negotiations

Introduction: Awareness is the first line of defense. Understanding common manipulation tactics enables sales professionals to prepare and respond effectively without being caught off guard.

Overview: Manipulation in sales can take many forms, including emotional pressure, misleading information, or undue urgency created by the other party to sway decision-making.

Case Study: A real estate agent recognized that a buyer was falsely claiming interest from other buyers to pressure a lower price. By confirming market interest independently, the agent countered this tactic with factual data, maintaining the price point and demonstrating the property's value.

Defense Against Common Manipulative Techniques: Gaslighting, Misinformation, Intimidation, and Emotional Baiting

Introduction: Each type of manipulation requires a specific defense strategy to maintain negotiation integrity and personal equanimity.

Overview:

- **Gaslighting:** Keep a detailed record of all interactions to refute any distortions or denials of what was previously agreed.

- **Misinformation:** Prioritize confirmation and fact-checking of any claims or data presented by the other party.

- **Intimidation:** Remain calm and assertive, using clear and firm responses to establish boundaries.

- **Emotional Baiting:** Identify when emotions are being manipulated, and deliberately steer the conversation back to logical grounds.

Case Study: A software sales director faced a client who used intimidation tactics during contract negotiations. By maintaining a calm demeanor and sticking to predefined terms, she demonstrated that aggressive tactics would not lead to concessions, eventually securing a fair deal.

"Silent Counter-Narrative": How to Mentally Disarm Opponents by Reframing the Conversation

Introduction: Altering the internal narrative about the negotiation can transform one's perception of and reaction to manipulative tactics.

Overview: This strategy involves viewing manipulative attempts not as personal affronts but as tactics reflecting the opponent's pressures or anxieties, thereby depersonalizing the conflict and reducing its emotional impact.

Case Study: During a high-stakes sales pitch, a team leader reframed a particularly aggressive negotiation as a test of his team's preparation and composure, not as a personal attack.

This mindset helped the team remain focused and composed, ultimately winning the client's respect and the contract.

How to Avoid Questioning Yourself When Under Psychological Attack

Introduction: Sustaining self-confidence is crucial when facing manipulation. Doubting oneself can lead to concessions and decreased negotiation effectiveness.

Overview: Regular self-affirmation, focusing on one's skills and past successes, and seeking constructive feedback from trusted colleagues can fortify one's self-esteem against psychological attacks.

Case Study: A veteran sales consultant regularly faced undercutting by competitors. By reminding herself of her extensive experience and previous client satisfaction, she confidently addressed misleading competitor claims, reassuring clients of her expertise and reliability.

Workshop

Activities

To transform the theoretical knowledge of this chapter into actionable skills, the following interactive workshop activities are suggested:

- **Scenario-Based Role Play:** Participants act out different negotiation scenarios to practice identifying and responding to manipulation tactics. This exercise helps reinforce recognition skills and effective responses.

- **Group Discussion on Real Experiences:** Sharing personal experiences with manipulation in sales provides insights and fosters a collaborative learning environment. This activity encourages peer learning and the exchange of effective counter-strategies.

- **Reframing Exercise:** Facilitators present challenging negotiation situations, and participants work in small groups to reframe their perspectives, focusing on controlling the narrative and reducing emotional responses.

- **Confidence Building Workshop:** Through activities such as crafting personal achievement narratives and positive affirmation sessions, participants boost their self-esteem, crucial for resisting psychological manipulation.

These workshop activities not only solidify the defensive tactics discussed but also enhance the overall resilience of sales professionals, preparing them to handle complex negotiations with confidence and integrity.

Conclusion

This chapter empowers sales professionals with the knowledge and skills to recognize and deflect manipulation tactics effectively. By building a robust psychological armor, salespeople can protect their interests and maintain the integrity of their negotiations, ensuring that they stay in control even when faced with sophisticated manipulative strategies.

CHAPTER 32

The Chess Master Mindset – Always Stay Steps Ahead

"

Adopt the mindset of a chess master: always thinking several moves ahead, where every decision is strategic, and every outcome is a step towards victory.

"

In sales, as in chess, strategic foresight and anticipation of the opponent's moves can define the success of your game plan. This chapter elucidates the "Chess Master" mindset, a strategic approach to negotiations that involves constant analysis, foresight, and tactical adjustments based on the behavior and potential decisions of the opponent.

1. Adopting the "Chess Master" Mentality: See Every Meeting as a Game of Strategy

Introduction: Embracing the Chess Master mentality involves viewing each sales interaction as a strategic game where every decision, like a move in chess, should be deliberate and purposeful.

Overview: This approach requires a deep understanding of the principles of strategy, an unwavering focus on the end goal, and the patience to make calculated moves.

Case Study: A tech startup CEO used the Chess Master approach in funding negotiations by strategically withholding certain pieces of information until pivotal moments, which maximized interest and valuation during talks. She treated each meeting as a chess game, where every question answered and information shared was a strategic move that led to a successful series A funding round.

2. How to Predict Opponents' Next Moves Based on Their Emotional Responses and Motivations

Introduction: Anticipating the opponent's next move is critical in maintaining the upper hand in negotiations.

Overview: This involves keen observation of verbal and non-verbal cues, understanding the emotional drivers of the opponent, and predicting responses based on past interactions.

Case Study: A real estate agent, through careful observation of a buyer's concerns about future family needs and emotional attachment to certain property features, predicted their preferences and hesitation points. This foresight allowed the agent to present tailored options that preemptively addressed

3. Scenario Planning: Thinking Two or Three Steps Ahead in Negotiations

Introduction: Effective scenario planning involves anticipating possible future scenarios and preparing responses in advance, much like planning several moves ahead in chess.

Overview: This requires a thorough analysis of the negotiation landscape, including the strengths and weaknesses of your position, the needs and wants of the opponent, and external factors that could influence outcomes.

Case Study: A pharmaceutical sales team used scenario planning in contract negotiations with a large hospital network by preparing for various objections and budget concerns. They developed multiple proposal versions and pricing models to quickly adapt to the hospital's feedback, ensuring they could maintain negotiation momentum and secure a contract.

4. Using Influence "Countermeasures" to Regain Control When the Other Side Has the Upper Hand

Introduction: Regaining control in negotiations where you're at a disadvantage requires the use of strategic "countermeasures."

Overview: These countermeasures could involve redirecting the conversation, introducing newinformation, or altering negotiation tactics to shift the balance of power.

Case Study: An IT services provider found themselves at a disadvantage during a service level agreement negotiation when the client pushed for lower prices. By introducing testimonials of long-term benefits and exclusive post-contract support services, they shifted the discussion from cost to value, regaining control and concluding the deal on favorable terms.

Workshop
Activities

To help internalize the Chess Master mindset and techniques, the following workshop activities are recommended:

- **Role-Playing Different Negotiation Scenarios:** Participants practice applying the Chess Master mentality in simulated negotiations, learning how to think several moves ahead and adapt their strategies based on the opponent's actions.

- **Predictive Strategy Exercises:** Teams analyze case studies and predict outcomes based on given scenarios, then discuss alternative strategies to handle each situation.

- **Scenario Planning Workshops:** Groups create detailed plans for hypothetical negotiation challenges, identifying key decision points and preparing contingent moves.

- **Countermeasures Brainstorming Sessions:** Participants identify potential negotiation setbacks and collaborate to develop strategic responses or countermeasures.

These activities not only reinforce the strategic principles outlined in the chapter but also enhance participants' ability to think critically and strategically in real-world sales negotiations, embodying the foresight and adaptiveness of a chess master.

Conclusion

Adopting a Chess Master mindset transforms the approach to sales from reactive to strategic. By anticipating opponents' moves and thinking several steps ahead, sales professionals can navigate complex negotiations with foresight and agility. This proactive stance allows them to maintain control over the sales process and consistently secure favorable outcomes.

YOUR MISSION BEGINS NOW

Sales is more than a profession—it's a discipline, a craft, and for those who master it, a lifelong journey of growth. This book has armed you with strategies inspired by many of the most disciplined and effective spy organizations in the world. These principles—adapted for the sales environment—are designed to transform the way you think, act, and lead.

What You've Learned

From building trust and mastering timing to handling resistance and leading with purpose, you've gained a comprehensive toolkit for success. Each section of this book has equipped you with actionable insights to thrive at every stage of the sales process:

1. **Understanding Human Behavior:** Learn to decode people, build rapport, and connect on a deeper level.

2. **Strategic Preparation:** Prepare like an operative with detailed research, anticipation of challenges, and tactical adaptability.

3. **Gathering Intelligence:** Extract the information you need to craft tailored solutions and build stronger relationships.

4. **Influencing Decisions:** Use psychological principles and strategic framing to guide prospects toward confident decisions.

5. **Operating in Complex Environments:** Stay composed under pressure, adapt to shifting dynamics, and turn challenges into opportunities.

6. **Closing Deals and Building Relationships:** Foster trust, deliver value, and create partnerships that last beyond the initial sale.

7. **Mastering the Sales Mindset:** Cultivate resilience, embrace growth, and lead with the discipline and foresight of a true sales tactician.

8. **Harnessing Psychological Insight:** Explore advanced psychological tools

The Sales Tactician's Creed

- **Be Prepared:** Success is earned through knowledge and readiness.

- **Be Insightful:** Read between the lines and listen for what isn't being said.

- **Be Adaptable:** Adjust your approach in real time to match evolving circumstances.

- **Be Ethical:** Influence with integrity and build lasting partnerships.

- **Be Relentless:** Pursue continuous improvement and never settle for less than excellence.

By adopting the mindset of a tactician, you'll no longer just react to opportunities—you'll create them. You are now equipped to influence, adapt, and thrive in the ever-changing world of sales. Success is your mission—now, go execute it.

Your Next Steps

1. **Apply What You've Learned:** Knowledge without action is powerless. Begin incorporating these strategies into your daily practice immediately.

2. **Refine and Evolve:** Treat every interaction as an opportunity to learn and grow. Reflect, adapt, and continuously improve.

3. **Lead with Purpose:** Whether you're guiding a client or mentoring a team, your influence has the power to create lasting change. Use it wisely.

The Legacy You Leave

Sales isn't about transactions—it's about relationships. By thinking like an operative and acting like a leader, you're not only closing deals but also building trust, creating value, and leaving a lasting impression on your clients and colleagues.

Your journey as a sales tactician is just beginning. Every call, meeting, and negotiation is a chance to refine your craft, push your limits, and make an impact. Like a skilled operative, you now have the tools, mindset, and discipline to succeed in any situation. The mission is yours—go out and achieve greatness.

The world of sales is waiting for a leader like you.

APPENDIX: FURTHER READING BY CHAPTER TOPICS

Chapter 1: The Spy Who Sold Me

- **Cialdini, Robert B.** *Influence: The Psychology of Persuasion.* New York: Harper Business, 2006.

- **Goleman, Daniel.** *Emotional Intelligence: Why It Can Matter More Than IQ.* New York: Bantam Books, 1995.

- **Gladwell, Malcolm.** *Blink: The Power of Thinking Without Thinking.* New York: Little, Brown, and Company, 2005.

Chapter 2: The Three Lives of Your Customer

- **Sinek, Simon.** *Start with Why: How Great Leaders Inspire Everyone to Take Action.* New York: Portfolio, 2009.

- **Heath, Chip, and Heath, Dan.** *Made to Stick: Why Some Ideas Survive and Others Die.* New York: Random House, 2007.

- **Zaltman, Gerald.** *How Customers Think: Essential Insights into the Mind of the Market.* Boston: Harvard Business Review Press, 2003.

Chapter 3: Reading People Like a Spy

- **Navarro, Joe, and Karlins, Marvin**. *What Every Body is Saying: An Ex-FBI Agent's Guide to Speed-Reading People.* New York: HarperCollins, 2008.

- **Ekman, Paul.** *Telling Lies: Clues to Deceit in the Marketplace, Politics, and Marriage.* New York: W.W. Norton & Company, 2009.

- **Pease, Allan, and Pease, Barbara.** *The Definitive Book of Body Language.* New York: Bantam, 2004.

Chapter 4: Building Instant Rapport

- **Brooks, David.** *The Social Animal: The Hidden Sources of Love, Character, and Achievement.* New York: Random House, 2011.

- **Carnegie, Dale.** *How to Win Friends and Influence People.* New York: Simon & Schuster, 1936.

- **Ury, William.** *Getting to Yes with Yourself: And Other Worthy Opponents.* New York: Harper Business, 2015.

Chapter 5: The Psychology of Connection

- **Kahneman, Daniel.** *Thinking, Fast and Slow.* New York: Farrar, Straus and Giroux, 2011.

- **Pink, Daniel H.** *To Sell Is Human: The Surprising Truth About Moving Others.* New York: Riverhead Books, 2012.

- **Goldstein, Noah J., et al.** *Yes!: 50 Scientifically Proven Ways to Be Persuasive.* New York: Free Press, 2008.

Chapter 6: Pre-Mission Planning for Sales

- **Rumelt, Richard P .** *Good Strategy Bad Strategy: The Difference and Why It Matters.* New York: Crown Business, 2011.

- **Covey, Stephen R.** *The 7 Habits of Highly Effective People.* New York: Simon & Schuster, 1989.

- **Ries, Eric.** *The Lean Startup: How Today's Entrepreneurs Use Continuous Innovation to Create Radically Successful Businesses.* New York: Crown Business, 2011.

Chapter 7: Open-Source Intelligence for Sales

- **Marr, Bernard.** *Data-Driven Business Transformation: How to Disrupt, Innovate and Stay Ahead of the Competition.* Hoboken: Wiley, 2019.

- **Babitsky, Steven, and Mangraviti, James J.** *How to Find and Use Expert Witnesses.* Beverly, MA: SEAK, Inc., 2013.

- **Porter, Michael E.** *Competitive Strategy: Techniques for Analyzing Industries and Competitors.* New York: Free Press, 1980.

Chapter 8: The Buyer's Profile

- **Kotler, Philip, and Keller, Kevin Lane.** *Marketing Management.* Upper Saddle River: Pearson, 2015.

- **Osterwalder, Alexander, et al.** *Value Proposition Design: How to Create Products and Services Customers Want.* Hoboken: Wiley, 2014.

- **Christensen, Clayton M., et al.** *The Innovator's Solution: Creating and Sustaining Successful Growth.* Boston: Harvard Business Review Press, 2003.

Chapter 9: The Art of Asking Questions

- **Grazer, Brian, and Fishman, Charles.** *A Curious Mind: The Secret to a Bigger Life.* New York: Simon & Schuster, 2015.

- **Marquardt, Michael J.** *Leading with Questions: How Leaders Find the Right Solutions by Knowing What to Ask.* Hoboken: Wiley, 2014.

- **Tracy, Brian.** *Sales Success: The Brian Tracy Success Library.* New York: AMACOM, 2015.

Chapter 10: Active Listening: Hearing What's Not Said

- **Schein, Edgar H.** *Humble Inquiry: The Gentle Art of Asking Instead of Telling.* Oakland: Berrett-Koehler, 2013.

- **Brown, Julian Treasure.** *How to Be Heard: Secrets for Powerful Speaking and Listening.* New York: Mango Media, 2017.

- **Nichols, Michael P** . *The Lost Art of Listening: How Learning to Listen Can Improve Relationships.* New York: Guilford Press, 2009.

Chapter 11: Elicitation 101

- **Schafer, Jack, and Karlins, Marvin.** *The Like Switch: An Ex-FBI Agent's Guide to Influencing, Attracting, and Winning People Over.* New York: T ouchstone, 2015.

- **Hendrickson, Clare.** *Persuasive Conversations: Psychology-Based Techniques to Influence and Engage Others.* New York: Business Expert Press, 2021.

- **Yager, Jan.** *Effective Business and Professional Communication.* Boston: Pearson, 2021.

Chapter 12: Deception Detection

- **Vrij, Aldert.** *Detecting Lies and Deceit: Pitfalls and Opportunities.* Hoboken: Wiley, 2008.

- **Hartwig, Maria, et al.** *Truth, Lies, and Deception in the Workplace: Detection and Prevention.* Washington, DC: American Psychological Association, 2020.

- **Ekman, Paul.** *Emotions Revealed: Recognizing Faces and Feelings to Improve Communication and Emotional Life.* New York: Times Books, 2003.

Chapter 13: The Power of Framing

- **Kahneman, Daniel, and Tversky, Amos.** *Choices, Values, and Frames.* New York: Cambridge University Press, 2000.

- **Ariely, Dan.** *Predictably Irrational: The Hidden Forces That Shape Our Decisions.* New York: HarperCollins, 2008.

- **Heath, Chip, and Heath, Dan.** *Switch: How to Change Things When Change is Hard.* New York: Broadway Books, 2010.

Chapter 14: Exploiting Cognitive Biases for Persuasion

- **Thaler, Richard H., and Sunstein, Cass R.** *Nudge: Improving Decisions About Health, Wealth, and Happiness.* New York: Penguin Books, 2009.

- **Cialdini, Robert B.** *Pre-Suasion: A Revolutionary Way to Influence and Persuade.* New York: Simon & Schuster, 2016.

- **Ariely, Dan.** *The Upside of Irrationality: The Unexpected Benefits of Defying Logic at Work and at Home.* New York: HarperCollins, 2010.

Chapter 15: The Storytelling Advantage

- **Simmons, Annette.** *The Story Factor: Inspiration, Influence, and Persuasion Through the Art of Storytelling.* New York: Basic Books, 2006.

- **Guber, Peter.** *Tell to Win: Connect, Persuade, and Triumph with the Hidden Power of Story.* New York: Crown Business, 2011.

- **Denning, Stephen.** *The Leader's Guide to Storytelling: Mastering the Art and Discipline of Business Narrative.* Hoboken: Wiley, 2011.

Chapter 16: Selling the Spy Way: Crafting Actionable Briefs

- **Pink, Daniel H.** *The Adventures of Johnny Bunko: The Last Career Guide You'll Ever Need.* New York: Riverhead Books, 2008.

- **Duarte, Nancy.** *Slide:ology: The Art and Science of Creating Great Presentations.* Sebastopol: O'Reilly Media, 2008.

- **Reynolds, Garr.** *Presentation Zen: Simple Ideas on Presentation Design and Delivery.* Berkeley: New Riders, 2008.

Chapter 17: Situational Awareness in Sales

- **Endsley, Mica R.** *Designing for Situation Awareness: An*

Approach to User-Centered Design. Boca Raton: CRC Press, 2012.

- **Goleman, Daniel.** *Focus: The Hidden Driver of Excellence.* New York: Harper, 2013.

- **Klein, Gary.** *Sources of Power: How People Make Decisions.* Cambridge: MIT Press, 1998.

Chapter 18: Handling Hostility and Resistance

- **Voss, Chris, and Raz, Tahl.** *Never Split the Difference: Negotiating As If Your Life Depended On It.* New York: Harper Business, 2016.

- **Rosenberg, Marshall B.** *Nonviolent Communication: A Language of Life.* Encinitas: PuddleDancer Press, 2003.

- **Patterson, Kerry, et al.** *Crucial Conversations: Tools for Talking When Stakes Are High.* New York: McGraw-Hill Education, 2002.

Chapter 19: Counterintelligence in Sales

- **Herring, Jan P .** *Key Intelligence Topics: A Guide to Using Competitive Intelligence for Decision-Making.* Annapolis: SCIP Press, 1998.

- **Kahaner, Larry.** *Competitive Intelligence: How to Gather, Analyze, and Use Information to Move Your Business to the Top.* New York: Simon & Schuster, 1997.

- **Janes, Joseph.** *Library 2020: Today's Leading Visionaries Describe Tomorrow's Library.* Lanham: Scarecrow Press, 2013.

Chapter 20: Leveraging the Power of Silence

- **Navarro, Joe.** *The Power of Silence: Why Leaders Do More When They Say Less.* London: Collins, 2019.

- **Mackay, Harvey.** *The Mackay MBA of Selling in the Real World.* New York: Portfolio, 2011.

- **Ury, William.** *The Power of a Positive No: Save the Deal Save the Relationship and Still Say No.* New York: Bantam Books, 2007.

Chapter 21: Trust is the Currency

- **Covey, Stephen M.R., and Merrill, Rebecca R.** *The Speed of Trust: The One Thing That Changes Everything.* New York: Free Press, 2008.

- **Zak, Paul J.** *Trust Factor: The Science of Creating High-Performance Companies.* Hoboken: Wiley, 2017.

- **Dirks, Kurt T ., and Ferrin, Donald L.** *Trust in Leadership and Organizations.* Thousand Oaks: SAGE Publications, 2002.

Chapter 22: Timing is Everything

- **Heath, Chip, and Heath, Dan.** *Decisive: How to Make Better Choices in Life and Work.* New York: Crown Business, 2013.

- **Pink, Daniel H.** *When: The Scientific Secrets of Perfect Timing.* New York: Riverhead Books, 2018.

- **Goleman, Daniel.** *Social Intelligence: The New Science of Human Relationships.* New York: Bantam Books, 2006.

Chapter 23: Retention as a Spycraft Skill

- **Goodman, John A.** *Customer Experience 3.0: High-Profit Strategies in the Age of Techno Service.* New York: AMACOM, 2014.

- **Dixon, Matthew, et al.** *The Effortless Experience: Conquering the New Battleground for Customer Loyalty.* New York: Penguin Random House, 2013.

- **Griffin, Jill.** *Customer Loyalty: How to Earn It, How to Keep It.* Hoboken: Wiley, 2002.

Chapter 24: Becoming Their Go-To Operative

- **Maxwell, John C.** *The 5 Levels of Leadership: Proven Steps to Maximize Your Potential.* New York: Center Street, 2011.

- **Hill, Linda A., et al.** *Collective Genius: The Art and Practice of Leading Innovation.* Boston: Harvard Business Review Press, 2014.

- **Berson, Alan S., and Stieglitz, Richard G.** *Leadership Conversations: Challenging High Potential Managers to Become Great Leaders.* San Francisco: Jossey-Bass, 2013.

Chapter 25: Operative-Level Resilience

- **Duckworth, Angela.** *Grit: The Power of Passion and Perseverance.* New York: Scribner, 2016.

- **Loehr, Jim, and Schwartz, T ony.** *The Power of Full Engagement: Managing Energy, Not Time, Is the Key to High Performance and Personal Renewal.* New York: Free Press, 2003.

- **Brown, Brené.** *Daring Greatly: How the Courage to Be Vulnerable Transforms the Way We Live, Love, Parent, and Lead.* New York: Gotham Books, 2012.

Chapter 26: Continuous Improvement

- **Kaizen Institute.** *The Spirit of Kaizen: Creating Lasting Excellence One Small Step at a Time.* New York: McGraw-Hill, 2013.

- **Collins, Jim.** *Good to Great: Why Some Companies Make the Leap... and Others Don't.* New York: Harper Business, 2001.

- **Clear, James.** *Atomic Habits: An Easy & Proven Way*

to Build Good Habits & Break Bad Ones. New York: Avery, 2018.

Chapter 27: Thinking Like an Operative, Acting Like a Sales Leader

- **Maxwell, John C.** *Developing the Leader Within You 2.0.* Nashville: HarperCollins Leadership, 2018.

- **Heffernan, Margaret.** *Beyond Measure: The Big Impact of Small Changes.* New York: TED Books, 2015.

- **Sinek, Simon.** *Leaders Eat Last: Why Some Teams Pull Together and Others Don't.* New York: Portfolio, 2014.

Chapter 28: The Framework of Influence – Spycraft Models for Sales Success

- **Robert Wallace and H. Keith Melton,** *"Spycraft: The Secret History of the CIA's Spytechs, from Communism to al-Qaeda,"* 2008

- **Allen W. Dulles,** *"The Craft of Intelligence: America's Legendary Spy Master on the Fundamentals of Intelligence Gathering for a Free World,"* 1963

- **Maria Konnikova,** *"The Mastermind: How to Think Like Sherlock Holmes,"* 2013

Chapter 29: Personality Decoding – Psychological Assessments in Sales

- **Don Richard Riso and Russ Hudson,** *"The Wisdom of the Enneagram: The Complete Guide to Psychological and Spiritual Growth for the Nine Personality Types,"* 1999

- **Don Richard Riso and Russ Hudson,** *"Personality Types: Using the Enneagram for Self-Discovery,"* 1987

- **Jo-Ellan Dimitrius and Wendy Patrick Mazzarella,** *"Reading People: How to Understand People and Predict Their Behavior—Anytime, Anyplace,"* 1999

Chapter 30: Emotional Warfare – Managing Your Own Emotions Under Fire

- **Travis Bradberry and Jean Greaves,** *"Emotional Intelligence 2.0,"* 2009
- **Dr. Steve Peters,** *"The Chimp Paradox: The Mind Management Program to Help You Achieve Success, Confidence, and Happiness,"* 2011
- **Daniel Goleman,** *"Destructive Emotions: A Scientific Dialogue with the Dalai Lama,"* 2003

Chapter 31: Psychological Armor – Defense Against Manipulation

- **Robert B. Cialdini,** *"Influence: The Psychology of Persuasion,"* 1984
- **Robert Greene,** *"The 48 Laws of Power,"* 1998
- **Jacques Ellul,** *"Propaganda: The Formation of Men's Attitudes,"* 1965

Chapter 32: The Chess Master Mindset – Always Stay Steps Ahead

- **Avinash K. Dixit and Barry J. Nalebuff,** *"The Art of Strategy: A Game Theorist's Guide to Success in Business and Life,"* 2008
- **Daniel Kahneman,** *"Thinking, Fast and Slow,"* 2011
- **Dan Ariely,** *"Predictably Irrational: The Hidden Forces That Shape Our Decisions,"* 2008

Thank you for reading,
and here's to your ongoing success!

About The Author

Mort Greenberg brings over 25 years of experience as a business leader, working with tech start-ups and major media companies. Rising from an Account Executive to the President of a division with 800+ employees generating $220 million in annual revenue, Mort has supported revenue efforts for various companies as they navigated the need for growth, mergers, acquisitions, and IPOs. He was instrumental in shaping the digital advertising landscape during the early days of the Internet at Excite.com and Ask Jeeves. He has also held leadership roles at IAC / InterActiveCorp, NBC Universal, Nokia, and iHeartMedia. Along the way, he launched two companies of his own, FitAd and MindFlight, and learned that start-ups are not always successful. Since 2016, he has been helping turn around distressed media properties into profitable companies for a global private equity firm. The #1 lesson he has learned in all his years is that by improving people's revenue mindset, business problems are healed, and teams are motivated through innovation that new revenue affords.

www.ingramcontent.com/pod-product-compliance
Lightning Source LLC
Chambersburg PA
CBHW052108030426

42335CB00025B/2895